FROM GALLUP

*Based on Over **100 Million** Global Interviews*

WELLBEING at WORK

How to Build Resilient and Thriving Teams

GALLUP PRESS
1330 Avenue of the Americas
17th Floor
New York, NY 10019

Library of Congress Control Number: 2020948698
ISBN: 978-1-59562-241-9

First Printing: 2021
10 9 8 7 6 5 4 3 2 1

Printed in Canada

♻ This book was printed on chlorine-free paper made with 100% post-consumer waste.

Table of Contents

"Combining strengths and wellbeing at work is potentially the most transformational treatment yet in the urgent pursuit of resiliency, mental health and ultimately, net thriving."

— Jim Harter, Ph.D.

Introduction:
The Mood of the World

What if the next global crisis is a mental health pandemic?

It is here now.

At this writing, the U.S. Census Bureau finds that a third of Americans are showing signs of clinical anxiety or depression. This is a huge jump from even before the COVID-19 pandemic. In a question about depressed mood, the percentage of Americans who reported symptoms doubled from 2014. Gallup also found historic increases in stress and worry across our U.S. sampling frames.

As anxiety and stress soar, so does hopelessness, too often followed by suicides — including "deaths of despair," a new designation made prominent by Princeton economists Anne Case and Nobel laureate Sir Angus Deaton.

Deaths of despair are suicides and deaths caused by fatal behaviors such as drug overdoses and liver failure from chronic alcohol consumption. They have increased dramatically since the mid-1990s, from about 65,000 in 1995 to 158,000 in 2018.

Think of deaths of despair as suicide in slow motion.

Gallup knows that a mental health pandemic can kill hundreds of thousands of citizens just as a coronavirus pandemic can.

In a 2020 worldwide survey, Gallup found that roughly seven in 10 people are struggling or suffering in their lives.

Besides destroying lives, suffering can destroy the human spirit that drives innovation, economic energy and eventually, good jobs. This is likely tied to declining economic dynamism. Global GDP per capita is slowing — it has been for decades. And so far, it has been impossible to reverse.

Declining economic dynamism is the other global warming.

Gallup is taking on the mental health challenge, because solving any big, seemingly impossible problem starts with the question "What can we measure?"

Metrics That Help Leaders Run a Better World

There are measures such as the United Nations' Sustainable Development Goals, which include the official statistics of worldwide poverty, pollution, hunger, modern slavery and disease. These widely recognized official statistics of the most serious conditions facing humankind — that world leaders know as "SDGs" — are mostly collected by governments, nongovernmental organizations and some by Gallup.

Gallup believes SDGs are a good thing that world leaders need, or they have no way of auditing societal progress. These metrics help leaders run a better world.

Environmental, Social and Governance (ESG) principles are another even newer set of measurables that associations such as the U.S. Business Roundtable and World Economic Forum are forming and agreeing on. And the Big Four accounting firms and large corporations are supporting these ESG standards. ESG principles are being built to help run better corporations.

Corporations are being asked to use ESG principles to expand their business purpose beyond shareholder return.

They are being asked to provide proof of a positive impact on the environment, as well as on the communities, customers and suppliers they engage. And they need to offer evidence that they operate with ethics and integrity (governance). These new requirements audit the character of an organization.

SDGs and ESG principles are good things. They demand more from leadership.

However, there are still no organizational benchmarks for the most critical issue of all — the state of mental health and wellbeing. There are no formal agreed-upon metrics for the states of suffering, struggling and thriving.

There are still no official statistics for worldwide workplace wellbeing.

It is unlikely that you or other leaders have data on companywide wellbeing or resiliency — or data on how many employees in your organization are filled with stress and will soon burn out versus how many experience high inspiration.

There are no official statistics for "How are your employees making it through COVID-19 and a crashing economy?"

We know the temperature of the Earth, and we closely monitor the increments of rising seas. We know that the moon is more than 200,000 miles away and that Mars is over 33 million miles away — but we have very few measurements on the mood of the world.

The best thing we have is crude global suicide data that offer *some* insights into suffering. The World Health Organization estimates country suicide rates, which gives us a general idea of the prevalence of this most tragic translation of life — extreme emotional suffering. This is about as close as it gets.

What we need is a way to check in on all constituencies in all countries and organizations so we can ask, "How is your life going?"

When a CEO, prime minister, governor or mayor asks, "What percentage of our people are suffering, struggling or thriving?" — just measuring and reporting the answers will change the world.

There are no official statistics for "How are your employees making it through COVID-19 and a crashing economy?"

Gallup Net Thriving

Gallup's goal is to discover and quantify the difference between the best possible life and the worst possible life.

The metric we used to report the *best possible life* is what we call "net thriving." Gallup researchers and our external senior scientists refer to this metric as "Gallup Net Thriving" (GNT). We have been closely monitoring Gallup Net Thriving since 2005. GNT is the "other GDP" for countries or the "other stock price" for organizations.

Gallup Net Thriving (GNT) is derived from this extraordinarily simple two-part question:

Please imagine a ladder with steps numbered from zero at the bottom to 10 at the top. The top of the ladder represents the best possible life for you and the bottom of the ladder represents the worst possible life for you.

BEST
Possible Life

Q1: On which step of the ladder would you say you personally feel you stand **at this time**? (0-10)

Q2: On which step do you think you will stand about **five years** from now? (0-10)

WORST
Possible Life

The Cantril Self-Anchoring Striving Scale (ladder scale) was originated by pioneering social researcher Hadley Cantril in his 1965 book *The Pattern of Human Concerns*. George Gallup included the measure in his 1977 classic volume *Human Needs and Satisfactions: A Global Survey*, and it has been tracked in Gallup's World Poll since 2005 in more than 160 countries, representing 98% of the world's population.

What the whole world wants is a good job.

Gallup recommends that every big and small organization in the world immediately adopt this metric to estimate and track GNT across their organizations and constituencies. Governments and NGOs are quickly adopting it now.

A GNT annual benchmark report is Gallup's 100-year gift to the world. For the next 100 years, Gallup will provide an annual "State of Net Thriving." This report will give you and the world a common metric and a common language to benchmark and share best practices.

Net thriving teams build new businesses and customers. They build cities and neighborhoods. They build parks and children's museums. They build friends and families. They build better governments. They get up in the morning and build things all day.

How do we build net thriving teams? One life at a time.

Our organization's founder, Dr. George Gallup (1901-1984), said, "There are 5 billion ways to lead a life, and we should study them all."

This is the moment to study them all.

In 2020, our society concluded that sickness and potential death by a coronavirus must be stopped at all costs. The United States subsequently shut down a $20+ trillion economy — bankrupting countless small businesses — and closed schools. All of this combined to put employees, families and kids in an unimaginable state of uncertainty.

This new state of uncertainty grinds the life out of people a little bit every day.

While the mood of the U.S. and the world remains in free fall, the right place to start reversing that mood is the workplace. One of the single biggest discoveries Gallup has ever made is this: *What the whole world wants is a good job*. People want a job that uses their God-given strengths every day with a manager who encourages their development. Stress and anxiety are most likely linked to "my job" (or not having a job). "My job" and "my manager" are the two strongest links to net thriving. In this book, we will emphasize and dig deeper into this finding.

Gallup research has revealed five states of wellbeing that we believe will change the world and human development forever. The five key elements of wellbeing are career, social, financial, physical and community — in that order.

Career wellbeing is first because Gallup finds that this element is the very foundation of "the best possible life." Everything starts there.

In the absence of a good job and career — which includes heads of households — there is no net thriving.

We can measure almost every monetary transaction imaginable over a person's lifetime. We know where someone spent their money during

---

The five key elements of wellbeing are career, social, financial, physical and community — in that order.

7

their 30,000 days on Earth. But there are few measures of how they experienced those 30,000 days.

It is not that we need to ignore or discontinue classic economic data to track humans. It is that we need to add data on *how their lives are going*.

The world needs a miracle. That miracle lies within the spirit of humankind. We have found a metric for you to use to track suffering, struggling and thriving — Gallup Net Thriving. We have found the treatment for you to use — the five elements of wellbeing.

We wrote this book to show leaders exactly how to create a culture of net thriving. If you and your team leaders don't change the world, who will?

PART 1:
What Is Wellbeing?

What Is "The Best Possible Life"?

Lessons From the Past

In 1958 and 1959, polling pioneer George Gallup and his colleagues conducted in-depth interviews with 402 Americans and 128 Britons who lived to be 95 and older. He called these people "the oldsters." The findings appeared in his book *The Secrets of Long Life*.

Dr. Gallup discovered what living a long life looked like decades ago, which offers clues to living a long life today:

- Respondents had jobs that required them to be physically active — 90% of men had jobs in which they were on their feet most of the time.

- 71% of men and 61% of women reported doing hard physical labor — their exercise came from their work.

- 62% worked outdoors.

- They lived in a time when there was little processed food. These oldsters were not particular about their food choices. They tended to eat plain cooking in moderate amounts — meat, potatoes and white bread on most days with *dessert*. They regularly used butter.

- Almost none tried to go on a diet.

- They were deep sleepers and early risers, typically waking up at 6 a.m.

- They worried very little.

- Most described themselves as "cheery" people who "take things as they come."

- They reported happy overall lives.

- Their main interest outside of work was family and friends.

- They laughed a lot.

- Most weren't intentionally trying to live long lives.

- They did not have luxurious lifestyles and were far enough away from poverty that they didn't worry about money.

- These oldsters' households were distributed across large cities, small cities, towns or villages, or rural areas.

- Half of the men never took vacations during their working years.

- The group's median retirement age was 80 for men and 70 for women.

- For men, the median number of hours they worked per week was 60. For women who worked outside the home, the median was 64 hours per week.

- 93% of men and 85% of women reported getting "a great deal of satisfaction" from their work. The majority of men and women reported having "a great deal of fun" at work.

What Can These Oldsters Teach Us Today?

By all accounts, these oldsters lived *thriving* — not struggling or suffering — long lives. However, no single factor guaranteed a long and thriving life — but the combination of several.

So what do Dr. Gallup's findings from the 1950s tell us about living a thriving life 70 years later?

We don't suggest using the list above as an exact checklist for today. After all, how many people have the option to get substantial exercise through their work, to work outside and to live a stress-free life? How many doctors would recommend a daily intake of meat, potatoes, white bread, butter and dessert? How many people are willing to forgo vacations and work 60-hour weeks until they are 70 or 80 years old? Currently, 78% of the world's working population is not engaged in their work — they are not getting "a great deal of satisfaction" nor "a great deal of fun" from work.

The key to a thriving life is not dependent on a list of policies or activities that everyone follows. Many of the oldsters' practices throughout their lives don't match the advice current experts recommend. Today, the tendency is to focus on easy-to-measure activities such as number of hours worked, vacations or diet. But the oldsters' thriving lives were better explained by how they *experienced* life:

> *They had a great deal of fun at work.*
>
> *They prioritized friends and family in their leisure time.*
>
> *They didn't worry about money.*
>
> *They ate in moderation rather than following a specific diet plan. They were physically active and slept well.*
>
> *They experienced little worry and were content regardless of the different geographies and town or city sizes where they lived.*

These findings are consistent with recent longitudinal research on aging and mortality.

When organizations attempt to legislate policies for transactions like hours worked, vacations and retirement that apply the same way to all people, they're missing the breakthrough.

We are not encouraging skipping vacations like half of the male oldsters did. We are simply pointing out that engagement trumps vacation time. Two people — one with miserable work and one with engaging work — have the most differentiated life outcomes.

Gallup's most recent global analytics conclude that a good job, with engaging work, is the very foundation of a thriving life.

While "my work" is the single most important variable, it doesn't exist on its own. Why did these oldsters keep working until they were 80? Because other aspects of their life supported and didn't conflict with what they loved to do. More recent large-scale studies reinforce this point: The elements of your life that affect your wellbeing are *interdependent*. There are five of them. They rely on each other.

Gallup's most recent global analytics conclude that a good job, with engaging work, is the very foundation of a thriving life.

Net Thriving: The Other Stock Price

Much like a financial audit, reporting employee engagement or Net Promoter Scores for customers has become a requirement for boards and institutional investors over the past two decades.

While employee engagement has been on the rise for the past 10 years, as of this writing, 36% of U.S. workers and just 22% globally are engaged. Engaged employees produce far better outcomes on everything.

However, Gallup recently discovered that engaged workers who are *not thriving in their lives* are much more vulnerable and add risk to your organization.

For example, comparing employees who are engaged but *not* thriving in life with those who are engaged *and* thriving, those in the former group report the following risks:

- 61% higher likelihood of burnout often or always

- 48% higher likelihood of daily stress

- 66% higher likelihood of daily worry

- double the rate of daily sadness and anger

Thriving employees have 53% fewer missed days due to health issues. Suffering and struggling employees have substantially higher disease burden due to diagnoses of depression and anxiety, among others. This translates into big differences in productivity.

Reporting employees' mental health and wellbeing will soon become a requirement for all organizations.

How many employees in your company are suffering, struggling or thriving?

If you want to know the wellbeing of your employees, this two-part question, called the Best Possible Life Scale, is the best question item Gallup analytics has ever found to measure GNT because it encompasses all aspects of an individual's wellbeing:

Please imagine a ladder with steps numbered from zero at the bottom to 10 at the top. The top of the ladder represents the best possible life for you and the bottom of the ladder represents the worst possible life for you.

Q1: On which step of the ladder would you say you personally feel you stand at this time? (0-10)

Q2: On which step do you think you will stand about five years from now? (0-10)

Your organization will need to know how your employees answer the Best Possible Life Scale questions to effectively meet the new demand of managing the *whole person*. Just like stock price is an indicator of current and future earnings, Gallup Net Thriving assesses the current and future resiliency of your workforce.

Even prior to COVID-19, work and life had become blended. Remote working and flextime were on the rise. And then with many employees ordered to work from home to flatten the coronavirus curve, work and life became *completely* blended for most employees.

Even with a vaccine and economic recovery, work and life will never be separated like they were in the past.

How Does Gallup Define "Thriving"?

Gallup uses the Best Possible Life Scale as the global standard to measure Gallup Net Thriving across 160 countries.

Packed into any person's responses to these two simple questions is almost everything in their life — from basic needs such as food and shelter to personal safety to a good job, social status, money and health.

Let's call the two parts of the Best Possible Life Scale "best life present" and "best life future." They are both important because one reveals your current state, which influences your decisions right now, and the other reveals your hope for the future. Even people in a negative state can keep going if they have hope that things will get better.

Gallup tracked wellbeing in 2020 during the COVID-19 pandemic, and the percentage of people who rated their lives highly on best life present dropped at a historic rate — while best life future improved slightly. People believed there was a way out.

Gallup analyzed how best life present and best life future predict happiness and health as well as negative outcomes such as stress, depression and burnout. Information from best life present and best life future gives us, in combination, indicators of whether individuals are suffering, struggling or thriving — an index of the resiliency of a culture.

Just like stock price is an indicator of current and future earnings, Gallup Net Thriving assesses the current and future resiliency of your workforce.

We determined the thriving, struggling and suffering categories based on analytics from over a million respondents across 160 countries.

- **Thriving:** These respondents have positive views of their present life situation (7 or higher rating on best life present) and have positive views of the next five years (8 or higher rating on best life future). They report significantly fewer health problems and less worry, stress, sadness, depression and anger. They report more hope, happiness, energy, interest and respect.

  Across countries, the percentage of thriving employees ranges from 8% to 87%.

- **Struggling:** These respondents struggle in their present life situation and have uncertain or negative views about their future. They report more daily stress and worry about money than thriving respondents do.

  Across countries, the percentage of struggling employees ranges from 12% to 77%.

- **Suffering:** These respondents report that their lives are miserable (4 and below rating on best life present) and have negative views of the next five years (4 and below on best life future). They are more likely to report that they lack the basics of food and shelter and more likely to have physical pain and a lot of stress, worry, sadness and anger. They have less access to health insurance and care and more than double the disease burden compared with thriving respondents.

  Across countries, the percentage of suffering employees ranges from 0% to 35%.

How Employers Can Improve Net Thriving

The first step is engaging your employees, because engaged workers are more likely to involve themselves in your organizations' wellbeing initiatives. Managers who engage their employees establish trust — making them open to wellbeing efforts that affect the whole person and issues related to suffering, struggling and thriving.

Work should be a stabilizing force in people's lives. This is particularly true in psychologically brutal times like those the world experienced in 2020. And employers play a central role in shaping the whole person.

The Five Elements of Wellbeing

Writings going back more than two millennia find sages such as Democritus, Socrates, Plato and Aristotle contemplating the ultimate purpose of human existence, which they called "happiness." So did America's Founding Fathers. Definitions of happiness varied from pleasurable sensations or feelings that you could achieve and then lose in a few hours — called hedonism — to the extent to which you live up to your full potential as a human being.

Everyone periodically reflects on how close their life is to "the best possible life." Psychologists call this type of life evaluation "self-anchoring" because each person can set their own criteria for the best possible life and rate their life at any given time. People make decisions based on how they evaluate where they are relative to their best possible life — what they buy, who they spend time with or whether they put their whole self into their work. The Best Possible Life Scale is an example of how to quantify the "remembering self."

Your remembering self is influenced by whether you have basic needs (food, shelter, safety), education, prosperity, employment, luxury conveniences or chronic health issues that limit your choices.

Ancient sages distinguished between the remembering self and more fleeting emotions and feelings. Let's call this more immediate, hour-to-hour and day-to-day self the "experiencing self."

Your experiencing self, for example, distinguishes weekends and holidays from weekdays. People report higher immediate enjoyment and happiness as well as less stress and worry on weekends and holidays. Moods peak on weekends, and the valleys start on Mondays and continue until Friday, when moods improve a little when anticipating the weekend. These ups and downs depend on many factors, including your workplace culture, quality of sleep and social time.

Immediate experiences also include interest, enjoyment, anger, sadness, loneliness and boredom. During the peak of COVID-19 in the United States, worry and stress spiked at unprecedented levels while anger and sadness did not. During the weeks after the killing of George Floyd by police in Minneapolis, anger and sadness jumped to all-time highs while worry and stress did not. Different life events trigger different emotions.

Your experiencing self is highly influenced by your family and friends; being treated with respect; learning something new; having an opportunity to do what you do best; and your daily health behaviors such as eating, sleeping and exercising.

Big and little events in your life influence, in one way or another, both your remembering self and your experiencing self.

For people with children, their remembering self — looking back — rates life better than those without children. The experiencing self for people with children, however, reports higher stress in the moment compared with those who don't have children. People tend to remember things differently than they experience them. Such is the complexity of wellbeing.

The remembering self and experiencing self are both correlated with income, but in different ways. For the remembering self, every doubling of income is associated with one point on the ladder scale.

But the positive effect of increases in income has limits. A landmark 2010 study of Gallup wellbeing data by Nobel Prize winners Daniel Kahneman and Angus Deaton found that increases in annual income up to $75,000 (about $90,000 in 2021 dollars) were associated with better daily emotions. Above $75,000, daily emotions did not improve. Furthermore, Gallup found that *how people manage and spend their money* has a big influence on daily emotions for people at all income levels.

Think of the two selves as representing two ends on a continuum often referred to as evaluative (delayed gratification) and hedonic (immediate gratification) wellbeing. Everyone wants to maximize both — to have the best possible overall life and the best possible daily experiences. Both are important to mental health and high performance.

Fortunately, there are wellbeing breakthroughs that show you how to improve your overall life *and* have better moments. Gallup meta-analytics uncovered five elements of wellbeing that do just that.

Employers play a significant role in affecting all five.

The Five Essential Elements of Wellbeing

Starting in the 1930s and continuing through the 1960s, George Gallup and his colleagues began using multinational polls to inquire about

27

various aspects of life on topics such as standard of living, health and perceptions of war.

Dr. Gallup led the first truly global public opinion poll from 1974-1976 covering two-thirds of the world's population at the time, including Sub-Saharan Africa, Australia, Eastern Europe, the Far East, Latin America, North Africa and the Middle East, the U.S. and Canada, and Western Europe. The findings were published in a volume titled *Human Needs and Satisfactions: A Global Survey* in 1977. The survey included a wide range of topics, from hopes and dreams of the world's citizens, personal happiness, job satisfaction, leisure, education, health, family life, standard of living, personal safety, the role of government, and women's attitudes toward housework.

Over the next three decades, Gallup researchers continued various studies of wellbeing, including community vitality and various in-depth targeted studies in specific regions such as China, India, the Middle East, North Africa, Europe and other parts of Asia.

In the U.S., Gallup has studied citizens' worries, fears and confidence during nearly every major crisis of the past eight decades, including the Great Depression, Pearl Harbor and World War II, the Kennedy assassination, protests and riots in the 1960s, 9/11, and the 2008 global financial crash — and in 2020, the COVID-19 pandemic and the unrest surrounding racial injustice.

In 2005, in partnership with leading economists, psychologists and other acclaimed scientists, Gallup explored the common elements of wellbeing that transcend countries and cultures. We conducted a comprehensive study of 160 countries, giving us a lens into the daily lives of more than 98% of the world's population. As Dr. Gallup did in the 1970s, we asked questions about all aspects of life. We then compared these results to how people experience their lives versus how they evaluate their lives.

In our initial research, we asked people what the "best possible future" for them would look like. We found that when evaluating their lives, people often give disproportionate weight to income and health. Across the groups we surveyed, "good health" and "wealth" were two of the most common responses. Perhaps this is because these factors are easy to measure and track over time — we can monitor our height, weight, blood pressure and income. Yet we do not have a standard way to measure the quality of our jobs and relationships.

Upon completion of the research, five distinct statistical factors emerged. These are the universal elements of wellbeing that differentiate a thriving life from a suffering or struggling life. They describe aspects of your life that you can *do something about*.

The five elements of wellbeing are:

- Career wellbeing: You like what you do every day.

- Social wellbeing: You have meaningful friendships in your life.

- Financial wellbeing: You manage your money well.

- Physical wellbeing: You have energy to get things done.

- Community wellbeing: You like where you live.

Gallup finds that the most important element — and the foundation for the other four — is career wellbeing.

PART 2:
Your Workplace's Wellbeing Opportunities

Key Points About the Wellbeing Elements

While organizations have a direct impact on employees' careers, organizational leaders are often skeptical about how much they should cross over into other areas of their employees' lives — and they should be. How much should an organization delve into someone's life outside of work anyway? Is it even appropriate for organizations to concern themselves with, say, an employee's physical health or community involvement? In thinking through these important questions, here are some points to consider:

The five wellbeing elements have an additive effect on performance and health. Gallup has studied this additive effect on several health and work outcomes. It seems obvious that working on your physical wellbeing would improve your health outcomes, but that's not sustainable on its own. For example, compared with those who score high on physical wellbeing alone, those who score high on all five elements report 41% fewer unhealthy days. Like stairsteps, disease burden, burnout, anxiety and associated costs are lower the more of the five elements you are thriving in. Having fewer of these negative outcomes frees people up to be better problems solvers and innovators.

Additive Effect of the Five Elements of Wellbeing

Career, social, financial, physical, community

Number of Elements Thriving	Net Thriving	Diagnosed With Depression	Burnout Very Often or Always	Experienced Anxiety	Disease Burden Cost Per Person
0	28%	37%	37%	44%	$7,208
1	53%	28%	31%	37%	$5,225
2	71%	18%	25%	30%	$4,766
3	86%	13%	15%	23%	$4,558
4	91%	6%	11%	13%	$4,112
5	98%	3%	9%	9%	$3,598

Findings after controlling for demographic differences
Source: Gallup Panel 2019-2020

Work and life influence each other. Most people spend one-third or more of their waking time working. Gallup's analytics and academic research show that there is a reciprocal relationship between work and life overall — that is, people take their work experience home and their home experience to work. Organizations demand a person's full energy at work. It is in both the individual's and the organization's best interest for people to thrive in all aspects of their life.

Wellbeing can be transformed. Some people seem to be naturally happier than others, and heritability studies do suggest that about half of individual wellbeing is due to genetics. These predispositions are often referred to as "set points." Your environment and your choices influence a wide variation above and below those set points. This means no one is doomed by their DNA. Recent research in the field of epigenetics even shows that the expression of DNA codes can be altered by the choices people make. So individuals have a lot of opportunities to change their wellbeing.

In a large global study, after accounting for demographic differences across people — their age, education, gender, marital status and income — we looked at how much variance in the remembering self we could account for. Gallup finds that net thriving can vary by as much as 70% based on how employees score on the combined five elements.

The five elements don't explain everything, but they explain a lot. There is enormous opportunity within just those five elements of wellbeing.

Which element is the most important? Individuals and organizations often ask Gallup where the best starting point is — *where will we get our biggest impact in the shortest amount of time?* This is a crucial question because neither individuals nor organizations can improve all five elements at once. The simplest answer is career wellbeing.

All things being equal, thriving in *what you do every day* makes for stronger relationships, a more secure financial life, good health and greater

Gallup finds that net thriving can vary by as much as 70% based on how employees score on the combined five elements.

community involvement. But the answer for where to start depends on where you are on each of the five elements.

At the low end of each element of wellbeing is a state of suffering. For social wellbeing, that is extreme loneliness; for financial wellbeing, worry and high stress; for physical wellbeing, chronic body pain; for community wellbeing, fear for personal safety. Anyone in one of these suffering states needs to be rescued on that specific element. But generally speaking, the best starting point is career wellbeing.

The five elements are intercorrelated — they are independent dimensions of life but also interdependent. In one experiment, Gallup gave people 100 points to spread across the five elements according to how important each element was in their life. We also measured their actual wellbeing on each of the five elements. Even though physical wellbeing was ranked highest in importance, it turns out that people who assigned an equal 20 points to all five elements had the highest overall wellbeing. Those who had an imbalance in points across the elements had the lowest wellbeing — in particular, when they gave an overabundance to financial wellbeing.

Focusing on just one area of your wellbeing usually leads to failure. It is nearly impossible to continually improve on any wellbeing goal if you don't consider the other elements. For example, who you spend time with has major implications on your goals to improve your eating habits and manage your finances.

Organizations that acknowledge and apply this interdependence can transform their employees' suffering and struggling into a culture of net thriving.

Career Wellbeing:
You Like What You
Do Every Day

- 20% of employees strongly agree that they like what they do every day.

- Those who disagree or strongly disagree that they like what they do every day report substantially higher daily boredom, more anger and lower engagement than those who strongly agree.

The Physical and Mental Suffering From a Bad Job

Burnout is now an official occupational syndrome recognized by the World Health Organization.

Twenty-eight percent of U.S. employees experience burnout on the job very often or always. And those employees are 63% more likely to take a sick day and 23% more likely to go to the emergency room. In France,

Germany, Spain and the U.K., 26% to 40% of employees say they have felt burned out in the last 30 days.

"I'm living for the weekend" is probably such a common phrase because so many people assume that work and misery naturally go together. Consider the employees who always watch the clock — putting in the minimum number of hours and meeting the minimum requirements of the job. Not only are these people unproductive — *they are also stressed out.*

To understand the experiencing self at work, Gallup, along with Senior Scientist Arthur Stone, studied how employees feel in the moment during their workdays. We wanted to learn about the momentary moods and physiological functioning of people in different work environments.

At the beginning of the study, we categorized employees based on their levels of employee engagement. Next, we equipped participants with digital devices using a process called "experience sampling." Participants were prompted throughout the day for each of three days — two were working days and one was on a weekend. With the digital device, they recorded what they were doing, who they were with and how they felt. We also collected saliva samples during these same moments to assess levels of the stress hormone cortisol.

Engaged workers reported higher levels of happiness and interest in the moment and lower levels of stress and sadness compared with less engaged workers. The differences were greater during working times than nonworking times. Moments of higher reported stress were associated with higher cortisol readings. Moments of higher interest were associated with lower cortisol. In the early morning as they were anticipating work, disengaged employees had higher cortisol levels than engaged employees did. There was no difference in cortisol levels on Saturdays.

Think about the potential longer-term toll of this repeated cycle of contrasting weekday and weekend experiences for disengaged workers. It's no wonder they can't wait for the weekend.

Interest Throughout the Day While Working

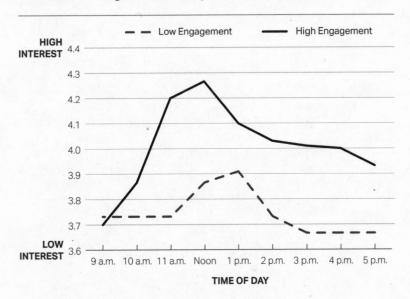

A large-scale review of publicly available data sources published in *Management Science* found that U.S. companies with high workplace stressors may contribute to more than 120,000 deaths per year and approximately 5% to 8% of annual healthcare costs. Workplace-associated mortality exceeds the number of deaths from diabetes, Alzheimer's or influenza.

Many employers have limited their focus on "wellness" to encouraging employees to eat healthy and exercise rather than focusing on the element that matters most — career wellbeing.

The bottom line is that many employers have limited their focus on "wellness" to encouraging employees to eat healthy and exercise rather than focusing on the element that matters most — career wellbeing.

Time With a Manager: The Worst Part of the Day

Spending time with their manager is the worst part of the day for employees, according to an approach called National Time Accounting that asks people detailed questions about their time use throughout the day.

Reviews of the academic literature find that abusive supervisors contribute to employees' drinking and drug problems, insomnia, and a wide variety of unsafe behaviors. Indifferent, uninvolved managers are problematic too. They cause emotional exhaustion and higher rates of active disengagement among their employees.

The good news is that organizations can fix these problems. They can dramatically improve their employees' daily experiences by upskilling managers to become highly effective coaches.

Moreover, when managers add wellbeing conversations to their management practice, it has proven positive spillover effects into other aspects of work. One study of nearly 29,000 employees in 10 industries and 15 countries found that in organizations where employees perceived health and wellbeing to be well-managed, organizational performance was more than 2.5 times greater than for those where employees rated health and wellbeing as poorly managed. In addition, those who said wellbeing was well-managed rated their organization higher for encouraging creativity and innovation.

Career Net Thriving

What does career net thriving look like?

An engaged employee wakes up in the morning thinking about the work they are going to do that day — and that work is interesting and challenging to them. They know they have the skills and talents to be successful. They enjoy the work as much — or more — than the paycheck. And they know that when they accomplish something, the people around them are going to notice and appreciate it. Ultimately, regardless of the stresses or demands on any given day or week, they *enjoy doing what they do best to make a difference in the world.*

When an employee is thriving in their career, their "live for the weekend" mindset fades or disappears altogether. The drop in mood from Sunday to Monday is essentially cut in half. These employees are more productive, creative and innovative because they find their work intrinsically rewarding.

Engaged employees work more hours. Their work life spills over into their personal life in positive ways. *People with high career wellbeing are more than twice as likely to be thriving in their lives overall.*

Organizations that care deeply about their employment brand will make efforts to set employees up for the next phase of their life when they leave the organization — their retirement or transition to whatever they define as the next chapter. Regardless of the stage of life someone is in, "what I do" is important and becomes their identity.

ACTION ITEMS FOR LEADERS:
Career Wellbeing

- **Make sure everyone in your organization knows their strengths.** Use a strengths-based strategy to design an employee experience — from attraction to hiring to onboarding, engagement and performance — that leads to a culture of high development.

- **Remove abusive managers.** No organization should tolerate managers who destroy the lives of the people you rely on to get work done. In today's workforce, bad managers are your highest risk.

- **Upskill managers to move from boss to coach.** Use proven methods to transition your managers' mentality from *boss* to *coach*. Think of this as a yearlong journey that starts with learning about high-performance teams. Each manager should become an expert at setting goals and providing meaningful feedback at least once a week.

- **Make wellbeing part of career development conversations.** Once they establish trust, managers and teams can dream big together — not just about career goals and development but about life and overall purpose and wellbeing.

Social Wellbeing:
You Have Meaningful Friendships in Your Life

- One in four people strongly agree that their friends and family give them positive energy every day.

- Three in 10 employees strongly agree that they have a best friend at work.

Employees are much more productive and deliver far better results if they have a best friend at work. This is one of Gallup's most compelling and controversial workplace findings. And it illustrates the importance of social wellbeing for thriving employees.

If organizations doubled the percentage of their employees who have a best friend at work, they would realize fewer safety incidents, higher customer ratings and as much as 10% higher profit margins. Contrary to old-school business thinking, friendships increase speed and efficiency. People spend less time second-guessing their coworkers' motives and intentions and more time having transparent conversations that lead to high productivity. Friends go out of their way for friends.

To illustrate the importance of social wellbeing at work, let's go back to the Gallup study on workers' momentary experiences. One of the questions we asked the study participants during their day was if they were with someone. If they said yes, we asked if they liked who they were with at that moment.

Employees with low engagement at work displayed a revealing pattern throughout the day. They started the day with people they liked; spent most of the morning with people they didn't care for; apparently went to lunch with people they liked; had a miserable afternoon with coworkers; and then, before ending the workday, joined back up with people they liked. You can imagine what the conversations were like during their more "pleasant" moments — complaining about the people they had to deal with the rest of the day.

In contrast, engaged employees had a more consistent experience. They gave high ratings to the people they were with *throughout* the day. The chart below illustrates these two very different days at work.

Liking Who You Are Working With Throughout the Day

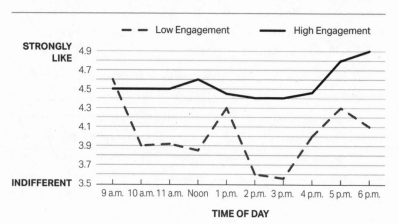

Because many employees were physically separated from their coworkers in 2020, the importance of social relationships was magnified during the COVID-19 pandemic. Humans are profoundly social animals — our lives are shaped by those we spend time with, whether at work or in our free time. From infancy to adulthood, our identity and personal sense of meaning are largely defined by our closest relationships.

Social distancing and remote working forced people to figure out new strategies to meet the basic need for human interaction: Zoom calls, team virtual happy hours, masked in-person meetings, for example. Without intentional efforts to socialize, isolation and loneliness become a big risk. Before the pandemic, social wellbeing was already the highest-risk element for remote workers. As of this writing, nearly one in four Americans report experiencing *loneliness* during a lot of the day. This figure more than doubles when people don't think friends and family give them positive energy.

Social isolation and chronic loneliness have a devastating effect on physical and mental health. Reports of diagnosed depression rose through 2020. Harvard Professor and Gallup Senior Scientist Lisa Berkman and her colleagues studied the relationship between social and community ties and mortality rates across nine years. People who lacked community and social ties had risks of mortality that were two times the risk compared with people who had many social contacts. These differences were independent of physical health, socioeconomic status and health practices.

In other words, the need for social wellbeing goes to your core. Many things can be going right in your life, but if you spend your days in a toxic social environment or without in-person interaction, it affects you physically and mentally. In contrast, people can withstand enormous uncertainty and suffering if they are part of a team that looks out for each other.

Social wellbeing is woven into all other aspects of your life. Even though there is a strong relationship between income and perceived standard of living, having strong career and social wellbeing substantially raises perceived standard of living across all income categories.

Social wellbeing changes how you interpret everything around you.

More Insights Into Social Wellbeing

You have a stake in the wellbeing of those around you. Extensive research has shown that health problems such as smoking and obesity are strongly influenced by the people around you — even those a few degrees removed. Your healthy choices are shaped by the people around you too. Social contagion of all kinds of behaviors is influenced by friends of friends of friends — meaning you are even influenced by people you've never met. In fact, research suggests that the people you call friends might have more influence on your health than your family history.

Studies have also found that the wellbeing of friends and relatives is a more effective predictor of your own happiness than the amount of money you earn. A Gallup study of people in the same households found that if someone in your household is thriving, your chances of thriving double.

Gallup longitudinal research has also found that people adopt wellbeing behaviors more quickly through peer groups. Thriving individuals are 20% more likely to have thriving team members. Peers have a major influence because they can measure and compare their struggles and successes.

Quantity of social time matters. Gallup has found that with every hour of social time, up to six hours, daily mood continues to improve. Social time, by our definition, includes all forms — from in-person to online to phone. Six hours a day is the average. The ideal amount will likely vary by person.

A "good day" for most people requires substantial time connecting with others. Across income categories, social time is associated with more happiness, enjoyment and smiling/laughter and less worry, sadness and stress. Generally, having relationships with more people is better. However, the quality of those relationships matters a lot too.

How many relationships do you need? People who have *at least three or four very close relationships* are healthier, have higher wellbeing and are more engaged in their jobs. In contrast, the absence of close friendships can lead to loneliness and depression.

Nearly all forms of social time count — up to a point. In a Gallup study, we asked 17,719 individuals questions about their previous day: how much social time they had, who they spent it with, what medium they used to socialize and how they felt during three segments of the day. We studied many forms of social time, including in-person socializing, emailing, watching TV, eating, exercising, social networking, talking on

Social wellbeing is woven into all other aspects of your life.

the phone and texting. We found that almost all forms of social time boost mood, but technological remote forms such as texting and social media have thresholds — mood drops after moderate amounts.

The best form of social time is in-person activities such as eating, drinking, exercising or walking. But there is an interesting twist — the total amount of in-person social time mattered less than the event itself.

Social time builds human capital. Traditional management may have discouraged socializing at work as nonproductive time. If someone is socializing, they must not be getting work done — *the office isn't a social club*. Some managers even frown on conversations about topics that are not related to the work at hand. At the extreme, leaders may discourage employee friendships — seeing them as sources of division, bias, gossip or office politics.

On the contrary, the right mix of social time actually builds human capital.

The key insight here is simple: People are intrinsically motivated to do much more for their friends. They look forward to seeing them, help them out when asked and ask them for help too. They have someone who recognizes their good work and who supports them when things go wrong.

Many organizations and jobs today are highly matrixed, requiring collaboration across several teams to get work done. This fast and creative work involves troubleshooting, problem-solving and thinking about how everything works together. Social time builds a foundation of trust that your organization needs for agility.

It is difficult for most people to achieve the six hours of social time they need if they don't get some of it at work. The difference in total social time between an engaged and a not-engaged worker is less than one hour.

Since being social is an essential part of human nature, people will find ways to socialize despite what their organization legislates. Do you want a culture of private gripe sessions? Or do you want to make the most of human nature and build a net thriving culture with people who trust each other?

As the 2020 pandemic revealed, some highly productive employees thrive on the social energy of people around them. Others appreciate periods of isolation to get lots of work done. And these people often work on the same team, doing identical work and performing at high levels.

Sometimes people prefer fewer, deeper and more long-term relationships. Others may prefer crowds, parties and constantly meeting new people. Some like one-on-one conversations; others prefer the energy of group interactions. But every individual has a need to feel connected to others. And those relationships are key for:

- engagement: Are your employees motivated to come to work each day?

- performance: Are they willing to go above and beyond to help their coworkers?

- wellbeing: Do they feel surrounded by people who care about them?

ACTION ITEMS FOR LEADERS:
Social Wellbeing

- **Include socializing in your onboarding program.** When onboarding new employees, make socializing an important part of their orientation. Everyone needs to know who their partners are and who they can rely on. Successful onboarding should lead to friendships and partnerships within the first year. Try to build in some in-person time during onboarding — trust develops much quicker in person.

- **Talk to your employees and get to know them.** Ask employees who they enjoy working with, who has common goals and who they would like to partner with on future projects.

- **Integrate.** Find ways to combine social wellbeing with your other wellbeing goals:

  - Career wellbeing: Publicly recognize your team's most productive partnerships.

  - Financial wellbeing: Encourage people to share ideas for reducing financial stress and building long-term security.

  - Physical wellbeing: Ask coworkers to share their health strategies and successes. People will connect naturally as they learn more about each other's processes and goals.

  - Community wellbeing: Use community volunteering as employee socializing time — encourage people to work together on shared community goals.

A few takeaways for leaders: No organization or manager can force people to be friends. While this element may seem like the most difficult for an organization to influence, it may be the easiest. While both remote and in-person socializing is beneficial, in-person interaction has the greatest impact on mood. But that doesn't mean you have to overdo it or that social connections have to drain time to be effective. Create regular opportunities for people to get to know one another through work. Then let human nature prevail.

Financial Wellbeing:
You Manage Your Money Well

- Only one in four Americans reported no money worries in the last week.

- Struggling or suffering financial wellbeing is the single strongest predictor of daily worry and stress for people with jobs.

Does money buy happiness?

Philosophers have debated this question for centuries. But it turns out this may not be the right question.

A better question for organizations and their employees might be "*How* does money buy happiness?" Regardless of how much any job pays, no organization benefits from worried and stressed-out employees.

Money is not an end itself, of course, but if directed at the right outcomes and managed well, it provides people with more choices and more freedom. And those choices determine the quality of their lives.

Earlier, when we introduced the remembering self and experiencing self, we discussed how the remembering self rates life higher at higher income levels. People in wealthier countries also report better overall lives. The experiencing self reports better daily emotions with rising income, but only up to a point. Above an annual income of $90,000 (in 2021 dollars), on average, daily emotions do not improve with increases in income. Consider these findings, however:

- A meta-analysis across 63 countries found that freedom of choice — autonomy — was a stronger predictor of wellbeing than sheer wealth.

- In a study of 17,820 U.S. residents, Gallup found that those who reported high financial independence — people who have enough money to do what they want to do — rated their lives the same on the ladder of life regardless of their income level.

The "oldsters" who lived to be 95 or older that George Gallup studied were not rich by traditional measures. They had enough money to meet their needs and rarely worried about being able to pay their bills. We find the same thing when we study people who have thriving financial wellbeing today. People can set up automated systems — automatic deposits into savings or retirement accounts or automated bill payments — so they can systematize good financial decisions regardless of their income level.

In other words, financial wellbeing is about financial *security*. Many people make a lot of money and yet feel financially insecure. They spend outside their means and accumulate credit card debt trying to keep up with or outdo their peers.

Others make a lot less but are financially secure, and they can do many of the things they want to do without worrying about money. That feeling is the core of financial wellbeing.

The *perception* that you have more than enough money to do what you want to do has *three times the impact of your income* on your overall wellbeing.

Interdependence of the Wellbeing Elements

None of the wellbeing elements operates independently — especially financial wellbeing. Consider these findings:

- One study found that 45% of Americans agree or strongly agree that they live "paycheck to paycheck." Employees who are troubled by their finances are twice as likely to be in poor health as those who declare themselves financially "unworried." They also report higher stress levels, more absences and lower levels of engagement.

- There is a compounding negative effect of health and economic stress. Gallup wellbeing data for 100,000 residents in 3,000 U.S. counties shows that economic stress has an even stronger negative impact on wellbeing for people who live in less healthy counties.

Employers should take this to heart. Although you may feel that you offer generous pay and benefits — or that there is little you can do to change them — your employees may be suffering from financial stress that is ultimately affecting their health and performance at work. Offering employees financial advice and resources not only supports engagement, it shows that you care about their wellbeing.

People will change jobs for increases in income, but their desire to move on isn't entirely driven by money. Gallup found that the amount of money someone will change jobs for depends on their engagement and career wellbeing. Actively disengaged workers will change jobs for almost any raise, while the majority of engaged workers would require more than a 20% raise to leave their current company.

Social and community wellbeing also affect financial wellbeing. As we noted earlier, the amount of social time people have on any given day improves their mood, regardless of their income level. Spending money on social activities creates long-lasting memories and deepens relationships, further boosting social wellbeing.

Once your basic needs are met, the best way to spend your money is to spend it on others. Spending money on others has been shown to be nearly as important to your happiness as your income is. Giving generously to your community, combined with volunteering, is a powerful way to increase your community wellbeing.

Your employees may be suffering from financial stress that is ultimately affecting their health and performance at work.

The Most Avoided Manager Conversation: Talking About Pay

Behavioral economics has recently revealed that much of how people think about wealth is based on comparisons with others. The amount of money you make or the size of your home is less relevant than how they compare to the income and houses of other people.

Now consider the fact that employees are more likely to believe they are underpaid relative to their market value.

A PayScale study of more than 71,000 employees found that when employees were paid above market value, 35% of them incorrectly believed that they were paid below market, 45% thought they were paid at market and just 21% realized they were paid above market. In contrast, PayScale found that of employees who were paid at market, 64% believed they were paid below market, 30% accurately believed that they were paid at market and 6% thought they were paid above market.

For this reason, you need to do more than simply pay employees at or above their market value. An open conversation about pay philosophies, policies and methods for determining pay is even more important than the actual amount of their salary when it comes to helping employees feel satisfied with their compensation. It's better to pay at market and have effective pay conversations than to pay above market but fail to align on those conversations.

ACTION ITEMS FOR LEADERS:
Financial Wellbeing

- **Provide financial planning, tracking, investing and savings resources and tools.** Ask internal financial experts to advise your employees. These experts can help employees reduce short-term financial stress, increase long-term security and use their financial resources to take care of basic needs.

- **Encourage long-term savings and retirement investments.** Employers can set a default into 401(k) plans, for example, where employees have to make an effort to opt out. Defaults increase the probability that your employees will do what is in their long-term best interest.

- **Train managers to have effective pay conversations with employees to improve perceptions of fairness.** These are some of the hardest conversations managers have. Give them the tools, support, information and education they need to set them up for success.

- **Use team incentives.** Consider how your incentive-based pay is aimed at team performance. Individual incentives can work too, but make sure you design them in a way that doesn't increase financial insecurity and work against team goals.

- **Consider employee wellbeing in your overall compensation package.** Including competitive benefits can increase employee wellbeing. Gallup's recent study of benefits indicates that they fall into three categories:

  - basics that are must-haves to be competitive, such as health insurance, 401(k) plans, paid leave and other insurance

  - benefits such as flexible working locations and monetary bonuses

  - benefits that differentiate whether employees are engaged and have higher wellbeing, such as flextime and opportunities for professional development

- **Encourage giving to the community.** Promote financial giving that is tailored to fit each person's passion and goals.

Physical Wellbeing:
You Have Energy to Get Things Done

- 75% of medical costs are due to mostly preventable conditions.

- About one in 10 Americans strongly agree that their physical health is near perfect.

- Two in 10 Americans strongly agree that they have felt active and productive every day in the past week.

The Risk of Poor Health Exposed in a Different Way

Most leaders are acutely aware that the trend toward poor health and associated costs in recent decades is unacceptable. At the same time, medical science has improved — with greatly advanced treatments for hypertension, heart disease, cancer and many other forms of disease. But these medical solutions aren't preventative. They happen after a condition has been diagnosed.

63

The coronavirus pandemic revealed how significant these chronic health risk factors really are. Even when treated, they present risks to resilience. At the time of this writing, COVID-19 was the No. 3 cause of death in the U.S., ahead of accidents, injuries, diabetes, lung disease, Alzheimer's and many other causes of death. It trailed only heart disease and cancer. But these conditions, along with advanced age and smoking, have been shown to substantially increase the risk of severe illness or death after contracting COVID-19.

In March 2020, at the beginning of the pandemic in the U.S., Gallup sought to approximate the number of U.S. adults at high risk of dying based on publicly available risk factors and Gallup National Health and Well-Being Index estimates of disease burden, smoking and age. At that time, Gallup analysts estimated that 11 million Americans were at severe risk of death if 100% were infected with COVID-19.

When the U.S. reached 3 million confirmed cases in early July 2020, the model predicted 132,826 deaths. The actual number was 132,309.

With remarkable accuracy, we could estimate the major role that underlying health conditions play in how resilient people are to a virus like COVID-19. Who knows if there are more pandemics coming or how long COVID-19 will have an impact on people's lives? But the lesson is clear. You can't change your age, but you can influence many of the other risk factors. COVID-19 dramatically exposed just how much poor physical wellbeing puts society — and your employees — at great risk.

As a leader, when you think about the new demand of a resilient workforce, you should think beyond cleaning supplies, plexiglass dividers and personal protective equipment for your employees. You need to view ongoing physical wellbeing as an essential part of your overall organizational health. Plus, struggling and suffering physical wellbeing also affect *daily* energy and resiliency. Your organization's ability to bounce back from a public health crisis, or any crisis, depends on how resilient your employees are.

The Immunity Benefits of Everyday Habits

At its core, physical wellbeing is about managing your health so that you have the energy to do all the things you want to do. You can have the most control over sleep, exercise and diet.

Sleep is a reset button for mood and immunity. Large-scale meta-analyses show, on average, that getting less than seven or more than nine hours of sleep increases the probability of many health problems, including hypertension, cardiovascular disease, stroke and obesity.

According to the CDC, 35% of Americans get less than seven hours of sleep per night, and only 4% get nine hours of sleep. So about four in 10 are in the unhealthy sleep range.

COVID-19 dramatically exposed just how much poor physical wellbeing puts society — and your employees — at great risk.

The benefits of good sleep are many: decreased stress, improved learning and memory, and enhanced problem-solving. For employers who need creative teams, sleep is essential.

Sleep also builds immunity. Fewer than seven hours of sleep a night takes a toll on your immune system. Medical research has found that people who have poor sleep efficiency and who sleep for too short of a duration were more likely to develop a cold.

And according to a 2016 RAND study in the U.K., workers who sleep fewer than six hours a night lose the equivalent of around six working days per person per year due to illness compared with those who get the recommended amount of sleep.

Everyone knows they should get a good night's sleep. While no organization can enforce sleep, leaders can communicate the research and teach managers to acknowledge its implications. Consider these findings:

- The brain uses 20% of the body's energy but is only 2% of the body's mass.

- While most of the human body clears waste from its cells continuously, the brain is the only organ that needs sleep to clear the waste out of its cells. Sleep literally clears the mind — providing a restorative function. Anyone who has taken a short refreshing nap or notices how they feel after a deep night's sleep can attest to this.

- In a Gallup study, we asked people about their quality of sleep the previous night. People with poor moods who got a good night's sleep bounced back to above-average moods the next day. But those who didn't feel well-rested were still in a poor mood the next day.

Exercise improves mood, immunity and learning. Ordinary people often need enormous willpower to exercise. Many struggle to make it to the gym or to wake up early for a morning run.

And yet much of recent medical research shows that even a small amount of physical activity (of any kind) boosts happiness almost immediately. In one study, people who exercised for just 20 minutes had significant improvement in their mood compared with those who did not exercise.

People who exercise are also more than twice as likely to feel physically attractive the next day. Even those who exercise *two days a week* are happier and have significantly less stress.

More effective than prescription drugs, exercising is also one of the best ways to combat fatigue. According to the Mayo Clinic, "A lack of energy often results from inactivity, not age."

Studies suggest that exercise also has an impact on the immune response as people age, on memory, and on the ability of the brain to form and recognize synaptic connections in response to learning — referred to as neuroplasticity.

Finding safe alternatives to exercise outside in natural light — for a daily walk in the morning, during a work break or in the evening — can also boost the immune system. While too much sun exposure can put you at risk for skin cancer, too little sun presents an immunity risk because your body produces Vitamin D in response to sunlight. Time spent outside is generally associated with lower chronic disease risk.

Exercise is important, but so is reducing long periods of sedentary time. A study of 6,215 adults found that sedentary behavior such as watching television or other screen-based entertainment time was highly related to obesity. Moderate to high-intensity physical activity was related to reduced obesity, but people who are sedentary for long periods (four hours or more) still had greater chance of obesity even if they exercised regularly.

For employers, these findings suggest that you can improve your employees' physical wellbeing — and their mood, immunity and ability to learn effectively — by designing workplaces and workspaces that allow them to get up and move around so they are not sitting for the entire workday.

Diet practices and "metaflammation." The history of nutrition science does not present a pretty picture. Plagued by special interest groups and misinterpreted findings, changing nutrition guidelines have likely contributed to high rates of obesity. In the 20th century, recommendations were made to move away from high-fat foods, which were gradually replaced with overly processed and higher-carbohydrate and sugary foods that likely contributed to the obesity surge that continues today.

More recent research highlights that calorie-rich Western diets, combined with sedentary lifestyles, lead to chronic metabolic inflammation or "metaflammation," which affects immunity. The dietary side of the equation is largely associated with processed foods, sugary soft drinks, fast food and other convenience items and snacks lacking in fiber, vitamins and minerals — foods that have basically had their natural structure stripped away. But the human body is designed to effectively process foods in their natural form.

ACTION ITEMS FOR LEADERS:
Physical Wellbeing

- **Reinforce behaviors that have long-term benefits.** Getting better sleep, eating healthy and exercising frequently have immediate daily benefits to building resiliency. Emphasize these short-term benefits to your employees to encourage healthy choices.

- **Make communicating the importance of physical wellbeing an expectation for managers.** Coach managers to share relevant corporate programs and to celebrate team members' personal wellness successes. And because there is a contagion effect, managers should model and recognize best practices too.

- **Make sure your managers and employees have the facts.** Ask nutrition experts who stay up to date with the scientific literature to summarize it in a way that can be easily applied. There is no end to nutritional advice from special interest groups or media who pounce on one small study. Amid all the noise, your employees need facts based on meta-analyses and randomized controlled trials.

Community Wellbeing:
You Like Where You Live

- Organizations with better corporate social responsibility (CSR) reputations outperform their peers on key financial metrics.

- Nearly one in four Americans strongly agree that the community or area where they live is a perfect place for them.

In Gallup's initial studies of the five wellbeing elements, community wellbeing stood out as a strong differentiator between a good life and a great life. People thriving in community wellbeing say that their life has exceeded their wildest expectations.

Why is that?

Similar to how a company's mission or purpose resonates with its most engaged employees, people get a great sense of fulfillment when they feel they are part of something bigger than themselves. Communities can give people that feeling.

People want to know that their life matters beyond work.

A meaningful job that makes the world a better place is important for your employees' wellbeing. People want to know that their life matters beyond work.

This sense of purpose is most powerful at the local level. No matter how digital society has become, people still live in physical places that form the foundation of their social lives. Just think about how the wins and losses of a local sports team can collectively affect the mood of a city or state — driving community pride and the economy.

Although you can communicate and travel around the world like never before, you have the greatest influence and leverage with those in your immediate community. Your "vote" carries a lot more weight at the local level. It is where you make the greatest individual contribution and where your time and resources make the biggest difference in people's lives.

Following catastrophic floods, hurricanes, tornadoes and other natural disasters, you often see community efforts to help those in need — because it's coded in our DNA.

A meta-analysis of 100 studies found that caring for the welfare of others is linked to higher wellbeing. But the researchers found that self-interest was also important. An individual giver's personal wellbeing is highest when there is some personal connection in addition to their altruism.

What's more, altruism improves longevity. *Well-doing* inoculates you against stress and negative emotions. A Gallup survey found that nine in 10 people reported an emotional boost from giving back and volunteering.

The New Leadership Imperative: Corporate Social Responsibility

Today's employees want their organizations to be part of a larger mission than just boosting profits and stock price. One in three job seekers say it is extremely important that their organization has a positive impact on the community. Organizations with better reputations for CSR actually outperform their peers on key financial metrics. As a result, CSR has become a leadership and board imperative because it provides a proven business advantage.

At a basic level, community wellbeing is about feeling safe and having adequate housing for your family. Many communities have major obstacles to overcome — for example, crime, fear, unemployment and pollution. It is impossible to get to the highest level of giving back when people fear for their lives.

In January 2020, the World Economic Forum published a list of common accounting metrics for consistent reporting and sustainable value creation. These are intended to measure environmental, social and governance (ESG) variables such as diversity, ethical behavior, health and safety, and greenhouse gas emissions.

CSR starts with organizations being good stewards of their organizations. However, the greatest benefits of CSR practices are when they extend beyond the organization to society at large.

As evidence, a meta-analysis of 52 studies published in *Organization Studies* found a consistent relationship between corporate social/ environmental performance and financial performance — in particular, the organization's social responsibility *reputation* in public reporting and from customers best predicted financial success.

Net Thriving: Community Wellbeing

Employees who are thriving in community wellbeing feel safe and secure where they live. They also feel like the place where they live fits the lifestyle they want. They take pride in their community, and they believe it is headed in the right direction.

Moreover, they give back to their community and make a meaningful contribution. At the highest level, they've been recognized for their community involvement. They experience the "helper's high" that spills over into the rest of their lives — boosting their mood, energy and inspiration to do good things in other areas of their lives.

Like the other four wellbeing elements, community wellbeing feeds, and is fed by, the other elements of wellbeing. Those with high community wellbeing have active lives, are more likely to be engaged at work and have more frequent social interactions. In the same way, physical health and financial security make giving and volunteering possible.

ACTION ITEMS FOR LEADERS:
Community Wellbeing

- **Be aware of the community issues that are most important to your employees.** People's availability and purpose change over time. For example, when employees have children at home, they may be more interested in programs that relate to kids. As life changes, so do opportunities for involvement.

- **Encourage employees to choose community programs that are personally meaningful to them.** Service projects can be great team-building experiences. But also look for ways for your employees to use their unique talents and expertise to give back. For example, a sales team might help raise money for a local nonprofit, or a marketing team could donate its time to provide graphic design or general strategy to promote a community event.

- **Give employees opportunities to share what they are doing in their community with coworkers — and reward their involvement.** Publicly recognize the community contributions of your employees and their teams.

Whatever your employees' passions are, it's all about doing *something*.

How to Build a Culture of Net Thriving

Most organizational leaders list "culture" as a top priority. They can count on a net thriving culture to bring high energy, innovation and agility to customer needs — in good times and amid crises. A net thriving culture is one that attracts top talent because it makes your employment brand — your reputation — something employees can *live*.

To develop a net thriving culture, first, it is important that your executives and managers are thriving in all five elements of wellbeing themselves. When your leaders are thriving, it spreads to the rest of your organization.

Next, those leaders and managers need to understand that the development of each employee is an end in itself. Each worker's wellbeing, and in many cases the wellbeing of their whole family, is dependent on the effective management of that one individual.

The world's best leaders get this. Former Ritz-Carlton President Simon Cooper told us how he sees the greater purpose of his organization as serving not only its thousands of employees around the world, but also their families. Leaders like Cooper have high awareness of the broader influence they have on their followers and whole societies.

To change a culture from one that is suffering or struggling to one that is net thriving, the key is making it easier for people to do what's in their best interest.

You would have a hard time finding anyone who does not want:

- an engaging career

- strong relationships

- financial security

- good health and high energy

- a safe place to live

Almost anyone's remembering self can agree that these are good things to strive for. But the evidence indicates that most people struggle to attain these goals. Why? What gets in the way? The immediate gratification of the experiencing self.

It is too easy for the experiencing self to separate a pleasurable experience *right now* from longer-term consequences. "One more cigarette won't kill me," the experiencing self tells the smoker — but the pattern will. The same can be said for hundreds of other destructive choices that eventually lead to struggling or suffering, such as:

- putting up for one more week with an abusive boss in a job where you are not developing

- neglecting time with friends and family because you're just too busy

- buying something you really don't need and maybe can't afford because you can put it on a credit card

- putting off exercise until tomorrow and sitting at your desk all day

- not getting involved in your community because you don't have time

It is easy for the experiencing self to say, "I'll make it to the weekend" or "I'll pay that bill later" or "I'll start exercising once things settle down." For the experiencing self, instant gratification keeps winning, and eventually wellbeing crashes.

For employers, this is particularly bad because it diminishes the extent to which your culture can deliver high energy, innovation and agility to meet customer demands. As we noted earlier, when people are struggling or suffering in their overall lives, they are more susceptible to physical or mental health issues.

The experiencing self can be the enemy. But it can also be the *solution*. There are many aspects of the experiencing self that align with the longer-term ideals above when the connection is clear. For example:

- An engaging job where you use your strengths every day improves your interest and enjoyment and reduces stress — in the moment.

- Time with a close friend, no matter how much or how little, increases your enjoyment and happiness — in the moment.

- Automating paying your bills reduces your daily financial worry.

- The endorphins from exercise improve your energy and mood immediately.

- Contributing to your community increases your sense of meaning and impact the very same day.

Making sure that short-term rewards align with long-term goals is essential. Organizations can play a big role in this. Here are some practices that any organization can adopt to build a net thriving culture:

- **Use the five elements as a science-based organizing structure for your benefits and wellbeing programs and offerings.** When you have a wellbeing initiative, align it with at least one of the five elements. Clearly communicate how it builds net thriving and reduces struggling or suffering. Use the names of the five wellbeing elements when you communicate wellbeing opportunities so employees can easily see how everything is organized to improve their everyday and overall lives.

- **Remember: Wellbeing initiatives that come from the CEO's office work best.** One of the most effective ways to improve wellbeing is to be surrounded by people who are making good choices. In an organization, it starts at the top. People often adopt wellbeing practices through social contagion, where peers learn from each other and their leaders and live the expected norms. Cultural change is an outcome of the expectations and the messages leaders send. For example, positive defaults make it easy for employees to do what is in their best interest (easy access to healthy cafeteria food, exercise, community activities, financial management, informal social groups). Keep in mind that the five wellbeing elements are interdependent. Programs and practices are most effective when they incorporate more than one of the five elements.

- **Equip managers to include wellbeing as part of performance management.** "Your wellbeing" should be an essential component of employee reviews. And employee development plans should include wellbeing goals. Managers are in the best position to know each employee's individual situation. This does not mean managers should play the role of financial adviser or life coach. It means they should integrate wellbeing conversations into their management practice and ongoing conversations. And they need to be able to direct employees to resources that can help them achieve their personal goals.

  See Appendix 2 for Gallup's Manager Resource Guide to the Five Elements of Wellbeing.

- **Develop a network of wellbeing coaches who collect and share best practices.** Organizations need experts, whether they are fitness coaches, financial advisers, nutritionists, or community service and volunteer organizers. The end goal is for employees to have resources and access to the best advice when they need it. The strongest nudges often come from peers. Every organization has influencers who are gifted at connecting others and encouraging involvement. Find and use your influencers.

- **Audit your practices and policies.** Most organizations have existing benefits and practices that are designed to improve wellbeing and promote a net thriving culture. Gallup has worked with many organizations to conduct both qualitative and quantitative audits to assess which practices and policies predict higher net thriving rates. Organizations should hold every benefit or practice accountable for its usefulness and impact.

Consider these seven accelerators of a net thriving culture:

1. **Rules and guidelines:** Do they work for or against thriving in each of the five elements?

2. **Communication:** Are your messages, especially from leaders and managers, consistent with a high-performing and net thriving culture?

3. **Facilities:** Is it easy to move around your office space, see outdoors and collaborate?

4. **Incentives:** Do they inspire participation in activities that produce results?

5. **Recognition:** Do you share and celebrate wellbeing successes?

6. **Events:** Do they build awareness of a net thriving culture and change behaviors?

7. **Development:** Do your development plans include wellbeing goals?

Be sure to evaluate your culture through the lens of the employee experience at each stage of the employee life cycle — attraction, hiring, onboarding, engaging, performing, developing and departure.

Building a culture of net thriving requires leadership buy-in and adopting practices that improve employees' lives — and is within the reach of every organization.

But there are risks to creating a net thriving culture — internal and external. We will review the four biggest risks in the next section.

Cultural change is an outcome of the expectations and the messages leaders send.

PART 3:
Risks to a Net Thriving Culture

The Four Risks

In 2020, organizational cultures saw historic threats.

It started with the COVID-19 pandemic and its immediate impact on people's health and lives, a crashed economy, lost jobs, and sudden radical changes in how work gets done. This was followed by record drops in the number of thriving employees and record spikes in worry, stress and symptoms of depression.

In the years leading up to 2020, it had become increasingly clear that stakeholders — including boards of directors, influential associations, institutional investors and governments — need a culture that serves the *person and society* as well as the shareholder. During the health and economic crises of 2020, meeting this cultural requirement became even more urgent.

However, designing and activating a net thriving culture that improves people's lives *and* performance demands far more than the traditional approaches of wellness programs.

The first step in building a net thriving culture is to avoid the four biggest risks:

1. employee mental health
2. lack of clarity and purpose
3. overreliance on policies, programs and perks
4. poorly skilled managers

Risk #1:
Employee Mental Health

All organizations should be concerned about their employees' mental health. This is especially true amid disturbing societal trends, particularly in the U.S.

In their recent book *Deaths of Despair and the Future of Capitalism*, Princeton economist Anne Case and Nobel Prize winner and Gallup Senior Scientist Sir Angus Deaton published a shocking compilation of findings exposing the first-ever three-consecutive-year decline in life expectancy in the U.S.

Behind this trend is a surge in deaths from suicide, drug overdose and alcoholism — primarily among working-class adults aged 45-54. This trend is predominantly among White non-Hispanics but follows a similar trend (minus suicide) for Black citizens decades prior. This extraordinary psychological pain stems from economic and social distress caused by the shift from manufacturing jobs to knowledge jobs, which are more likely to demand a bachelor's degree — and can be seen as more valuable.

The story is, of course, more complicated.

Case and Deaton hypothesize that this disturbing trend comes from lost status in society and loss of hope for the future — economically and socially. This particular age and education segment of the population has essentially been stripped of the pride and identity associated with "what I do." This lack of pride then cascades to their marriage, parenting, other social activities and standing in the community. These individuals, then, are more likely to turn to drugs, including easily acquired opioids and alcohol, to medicate the pain — sometimes deteriorating their health to the point of death.

Consider these other studies:

The English Longitudinal Study of Ageing found that subjective social status is associated with cardiovascular disease, cancer and overall mortality. A one-point decline on a 10-point social status scale accounts for a 24% increase in mortality risk for people aged 50-64.

A meta-analysis of 300 studies published in *Psychological Bulletin* found evidence that chronic stress is associated with suppression of the immune response in otherwise healthy patients.

A landmark study published in *The Economic Journal* revealed that prolonged unemployment of a year or more is one major life event from which people do not fully recover within five years. This study followed 130,000 people for several decades, allowing researchers to look at how major life events such as marriage, divorce, birth of a child or death of a spouse affect life satisfaction over time.

Wellbeing actually recovers more rapidly from the death of a spouse than it does from a sustained period of unemployment.

The Impact on Wellbeing
In the years before and after the event

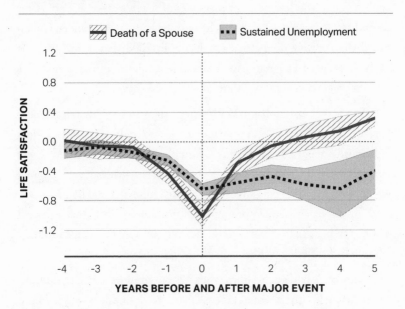

Adapted from Clark, et al., *The Economic Journal*, June 2008

But the unemployed aren't the only ones who battle these mental health problems. People who have jobs are at risk of emotional problems too. In Germany and in the U.S., Gallup found that people with a bad manager had even worse wellbeing than those without jobs.

During the 2008-2009 recession, Gallup studied new incidence of depression and anxiety across 9,561 employed respondents from the Gallup Panel who had no prior diagnosis of depression or anxiety. After controlling for age, marital status, income, education and gender, Gallup found that actively disengaged employees in 2008 were about twice as likely as engaged employees to report new incidence of depression (2.1 times more) and anxiety (1.7 times more) in 2009.

This is a global problem. With rising stress and suicide rates among Japanese workers, the government mandated employers to conduct individually reported stress tests of employees. Gallup studied 2,442 Japanese workers and found that stress was particularly high among young and unmarried employees who worked more than 60 hours a week. Actively disengaged employees were 3.8 times more likely than engaged workers to have high stress. Those who were actively disengaged in their job *and* had suffering wellbeing had the highest rates of stress.

During Gallup studies throughout 2020, employees reported record spikes in worry and stress amid the COVID-19 outbreak as well as record spikes in anger and sadness in the weeks following the killing of George Floyd and the subsequent societal unrest. Diagnosed depression rates continued to rise throughout the year, particularly among the unemployed and those working from home. According to the U.S. Census Bureau, Americans were more than three times as likely to report symptoms of anxiety or depressive disorder — or both — compared with 2019 estimates.

Among the employed, from March to July of 2020, Gallup found that the percentage of those who reported a lot of stress the day before ranged from 54%-65%, sadness 21%-36%, worry 43%-61%, anger 20%-40%, boredom 29%-46%, loneliness 18%-26% and anxiety 35%-42%. But employees who were engaged in their work reported substantially fewer negative emotions, even during these tough times.

In Germany and in the U.S., Gallup found that people with a bad manager had even worse wellbeing than those without jobs.

From 2006-2017, Gallup tracked the rate of dropping out of the workforce for 36,912 U.S. workers. After excluding those who stopped working due to retirement and studying a large number of variables — including race, age, gender, income, education, physical pain, prescribed pain medication, anxiety, diagnosed depression, job type, region, length of service, life evaluation and engagement at work (all prior to dropping out) — Gallup found that the top predictors of dropping out the workforce the following year were length of service in the prior job and disengagement at work.

There are many factors, of course, that are significantly related to dropping out of the workforce, as Case and Deaton detail. The catalyst appears to be the combination of *having a bad job for a long time.*

This series of studies highlights the immense significance of career wellbeing as a foundation for a thriving life. Career wellbeing touches all aspects of your employees' lives, including their relationships, finances, health and standing in the community.

While many organizations show concern for their employees' mental health, the solution — particularly amid these alarming trends — isn't just to send people to an employee assistance program. That is an after-the-fact response. Emotional health issues can have many causes, including predisposed traits. But the quality of the workplace is one factor leaders *can* control.

Risk #2:
Lack of Clarity and Purpose

Leaders in many organizations think they have checked the box on this risk to a net thriving culture. They have articulated a list of company values, a mission statement and even a vision for what the organization can become. But as many have found, simply writing and communicating these ideals does not mean they will be activated throughout the organization. In fact, only 22% of U.S. employees strongly agree that their company's leaders have a clear direction for the organization. Workers Gallup surveyed in France, Germany, Spain and the U.K. in 2020 also report low percentages of strong agreement with this item. Without a strong culture, the best intentions fail.

A strong culture is also essential for organic growth. According to the National Association of Corporate Directors (NACD) Blue Ribbon Commission, "Culture should be viewed as an asset, similar to an organization's human, physical, intellectual, technological, and other assets."

Creating a strong culture is the responsibility of the board and the governance committee as much as the CEO because the board owns the long-term success of the organization. Yet today, culture discussions typically reach the boardroom only when there is a problem or a crisis.

Only 22% of U.S. employees strongly agree that their company's leaders have a clear direction for the organization.

Recent scandals and injustices related to the #MeToo movement and racial inequality, as well as alarming compliance breaches, have brought culture to the forefront, demonstrating that the board is usually the last to know what the employees know.

Gallup recently reviewed the publicly available values statements from the 110 largest U.S. organizations, and they were remarkably similar. A content analysis revealed that, with high frequency, companies listed values such as integrity and honesty, respect, diversity and inclusion, customer focus and centricity, collaboration, and innovation. Who wouldn't want to aspire to these well-intentioned values?

And yet only 27% of employees strongly believe in their company's values.

To illustrate further, Gallup also asked a random sample of leaders and employees to provide words and phrases that describe their organization's purpose. Leaders were more likely to use words like *service, customers, quality, community* and *people.* Employees were more likely to use words describing their job functions such as *sell, teach* or *healthcare.* Leaders' aspirational purpose is not reaching the front lines.

At an even more basic level, in the general working population, only 41% of employees strongly agree that they know what their company stands for and what differentiates it from competitors.

Why aren't all the well-intended messages of organizational values, mission and vision statements resonating with employees? One word: *trust.*

Only one in three employees in Gallup's global database strongly agree that they trust the leadership of their organization. Levels of trust in leadership differ greatly across organizations — from seven in 10 employees who have high trust on the high end of the continuum to only one in 10 on the low end. Employees who trust their leadership are twice as likely to report clarity in what their organization stands for and to believe in the organization's values. They are also more likely to report that their company cares about their *wellbeing*.

Trust in leadership spreads throughout successful organizations. Consider the consequences of these two types of organizational cultures:

- **High trust:** Employees who trust leadership are twice as likely to say that they will be with their company one year from now. Beyond the advantages of retaining employees, high-trust organizations benefit enormously in the speed with which new initiatives take hold. And even when periodic mistakes in decision-making or communication occur in these organizations, employees give leaders the benefit of the doubt.

- **Low trust:** When employees don't trust leadership, they actively plan their exit while ignoring or half-heartedly completing their work obligations. They have no interest in making new strategies work or creating new customer initiatives. There is nothing in it for them because they've already mentally checked out.

In the age of social media, what happens within an organization spreads quickly, and this affects your employment brand and your organization's ability to attract star employees. Who wants to join, stay and give their best to a company with leaders people don't trust? And who really pays attention to or acknowledges mission statements, visions or organizational values as authentic if they come from leaders that employees constantly second-guess?

The big question is: What causes people to trust their leaders in the first place? Gallup's workplace analytics team dug deeper into our database of 4 million work teams and found this: The range in how organizational leaders are perceived — across teams *within* the average organization — was nearly as wide as the variability in teams *across all organizations*. Even though teams within organizations have the same leaders, those teams perceive those leaders very differently. Same company, vastly different perceptions.

A major challenge for leaders of large organizations is that there is no common culture — often even in prominent, highly regarded firms. This is true regardless of those organizations' lofty mission statements that are written to unite all employees toward a common purpose.

Most of the differences in perceptions of organizational leaders across teams in the same organization are determined by how each team perceives its front-line manager. Of course, leaders' consistency, clarity and ethics play a big role. But in large organizations, leaders have minimal direct influence on individual employees.

When Gallup asked employees to provide words or phrases that describe their culture, engaged employees used words like *friendly*, *supportive*, *collaborative* and *integrity*. Disengaged employees used words like *lazy*, *disorganized* and *slow*.

As Gallup highlighted in our book *It's the Manager*, a leader's success depends on their reputation extending beyond their closest confidants. There is a ripple effect in successful organizations: The reputation of leaders extends to managers, which then extends to the front line. Trust passes through these channels — but trust can't be left to chance.

So, who ultimately fosters trust in all levels of the organization? *It's the manager.* The reputations of your organizational leaders are filtered through the experiences of your managers. *Unfortunately, managers report higher stress and burnout than those they manage* — and a net thriving overall culture can't exist if managers are not thriving.

In short, while there is no common culture in most organizations, *there can be* if organizations develop great managers and give them exceptional experiences.

To increase clarity and purpose in your culture, you need to fulfill these basic requirements:

1. **Clarify your purpose and brand.** In the workplace of the future, your employment brand will be more important than ever. The new workforce expects their employer to improve their overall lives, not just give them a job. If having a net thriving culture is a priority in your organization, it starts with your CEO and board members. It also starts with a belief and stated mission that your organization can have more impact on your customers and society if all your employees have the opportunity to improve their lives in all five wellbeing elements. Your workforce will lose trust in your stated purpose if you send signals through pay, perks and lack of accountability that executives and shareholders matter at the expense of others.

2. **Make sure your managers are thriving.** Research findings suggest a contagion effect: When a manager is thriving in wellbeing, their direct reports are 15% more likely to have thriving wellbeing. Yet most managers report high levels of stress and burnout. They're often stuck between organizational decisions and front-line implementation. Most became managers because they are highly tenured or were strong individual contributors — criteria that don't naturally equip them for dealing with the complexities of managing people. To have thriving wellbeing, employees need a coach who makes their job inspiring and fulfilling.

3. **Reposition your managers as coaches.** Managers and employees no longer thrive in the traditional top-down, command-and-control "boss" culture. When managers are taught coaching skills — which include collaborative goal setting, ongoing feedback and accountability — they will develop high levels of trust with their employees. This is important because it opens the door for wellbeing conversations, which can include sensitive topics that demand a high level of trust.

If it were possible to legislate culture through policies, programs and perks, most organizations wouldn't have any culture problems.

Risk #3:

Overreliance on Policies, Programs and Perks

Every organization needs policies — standards and guidelines for how work gets done. Some policies are designed to protect people from accidents, others from discrimination or harassment, others to reduce lawsuits, and still others to improve worker wellbeing. Programs are often designed to teach employees organizational norms, to improve skills or to increase compliance. Perks are offered to enhance wellbeing, to attract future employees or to keep employees from leaving. But even with the best of intentions, some organizational leaders have misdiagnosed these as solutions for improving net thriving.

If it were possible to legislate culture through policies, programs and perks, most organizations wouldn't have any culture problems.

Anytime your organization designs a policy or program, you send a message about what you value and your culture.

Here are some findings to consider:

Working from home. Based on the composition of the workforce prior to COVID-19, economists estimate that over one-half to two-thirds of jobs cannot be performed from home. Among employees with jobs that *can* be performed from home, during the pandemic, about half reported a new preference for working from home, and 58% of managers say they will allow more remote work.

Gallup research indicates that employees with hybrid jobs — in which they can work from home some of the time but still perform work on-site — have the highest engagement. Working remotely brings freedom, but it also creates a management challenge: People who work from home nearly all the time report receiving much less meaningful feedback from their managers than those who work remotely part of the time. Those who worked from home nearly all the time during the pandemic of 2020 reported higher burnout. Gallup estimates that the quality of managing has, conservatively, two to three times the impact on engagement and productivity than any specific remote-work policy.

Hours worked. Many approaches to working-hour policies have been designed and implemented, including experiments with the four-day workweek, organizational bans on weekend work and even national laws restricting working hours to 35 hours per week. While there are differing reasons for these policies, they share the implied assumption that work and life are not well-balanced unless employees' working hours are restricted.

A Gallup analysis of working populations in seven regions of the world found that for people with low job satisfaction and no opportunity to do what they do best, increasing the number of hours they worked led to declines in life evaluations and daily experiences. But the result is very different among employees with high job satisfaction and an opportunity to do what they do best every day. Daily experiences and life evaluations did not substantially deteriorate when the number of hours they worked per day increased from five to 10.

The quality of an employee's work experience has three times the impact on their overall wellbeing as the number of hours they work.

Mobile technology use. Given the massive increase in the use of mobile technology, some organizations expect employees to use their personal mobile devices for work during traditional nonworking hours. Those who said they were expected to use their personal devices for work outside normal work hours reported more stress than those who did not. But engaged employees who were expected to use their personal devices for work outside normal working hours reported similar levels of stress as those who were not. High engagement is an antidote to stress.

Vacation time. People build up tenure to increase the number of vacation days or weeks they get. Vacations play an important role for organizations. They reduce dependence on any one associate and give employees a break from work. They are primarily intended to improve overall wellbeing. In fact, people with more vacation time, controlling for other factors, including income, report higher wellbeing.

The quality of an employee's work experience has three times the impact on their overall wellbeing as the number of hours they work.

But engaged employees who have less than one week of vacation report 25% higher wellbeing than actively disengaged employees who have six weeks or more of vacation. Having engaging work has five times the impact on wellbeing as the number of weeks of vacation.

Diversity and inclusion training. In response to inequities in organizations — primarily regarding race and gender disparities in hiring, succession and treatment — a variety of courses have been developed, including unconscious bias training. The impact of these programs has been reviewed through meta-analysis and suggests mixed results. While there is some evidence that these trainings increase awareness, *there is no clear evidence that they result in behavioral change.* Many of these programs are one-day or one-time events rather than being integrated into ongoing education for managers and leaders.

In many cases, perceptions of discrimination or harassment have cultural underpinnings that reflect the quality of management. For example, having a high percentage of employees who disagree or strongly disagree that they are treated with respect at work is a warning sign that there may be even more harmful issues in the organization. Ninety percent of employees who feel disrespected say they have experienced some type of discrimination or harassment at work.

Gallup has found that to have an inclusive culture, your employees need these three basic requirements:

- They feel they are treated with respect.
- They are valued for their strengths.
- They believe leadership will do what is right.

Ethics and compliance training. Ethics and compliance training is often, rightfully, required for government and legal standards. Doing the right thing is a business necessity. Organizations spend billions of dollars on litigation each year — and the cost of lawsuits has risen significantly over time.

Ethics and compliance issues quickly become safety, trust, productivity, legal, culture and brand issues. About one in five U.S. employees disagree or strongly disagree that their employer would do what is right if they raised a concern about ethics and integrity. This number shrinks to 2% when workers are engaged.

Further, Gallup asked 13,583 respondents if they have completed ethics and compliance training recently. Sixty percent said they had, but only 23% rated it as excellent.

Wellness programs. Many employers have hopped aboard the wellness bandwagon in the past decade or more, recognizing that they can play an influential role in helping employees curtail unhealthy behaviors that can lead to costly chronic conditions. A RAND Corporation study found that the likelihood of providing some sort of workplace wellness program ranged from 85% to 91% among U.S. companies that employ 1,000 people or more. It's safe to assume that these companies genuinely want to help their employees lead healthier lives while seeing a healthier bottom line too.

Yet simply offering a wellness program — no matter how well-intentioned — is no guarantee of improving your employees' wellbeing. Workers must be aware the program exists and be encouraged to use it. While more than 85% of large employers offer a wellness program, Gallup research shows that only 60% of U.S. employees are aware their company offers a wellness program — and only 40% of those who are aware of the program say they actually participate in it. Of the companies that offer wellness programs, only 24% of employees are participating. And engaged workers are 28% more likely than average employees to participate in a wellness program offered by their company.

Literature reviews on the efficacy of wellness programs show mixed results. The impact depends largely on the quality and nuances of the program and, importantly, the underlying organizational culture.

Pingpong tables and latte machines. Extra perks such as free lunches and take-your-dog-to-work days are fun for many employees. And playing pingpong with your coworkers may indeed bring some social connectedness, which is important for engagement. But these perks are not actually among the top priorities for the new workforce. When Gallup asked millennials which factors are most important in choosing an employer, "opportunities to learn and grow" topped the list.

Simply offering a wellness program — no matter how well-intentioned — is no guarantee of improving your employees' wellbeing.

Risk #4:
Poorly Skilled Managers

Of the four risks, poorly skilled managers are the greatest risk. Managers are the single most important factor in the engagement and performance of your workforce. They are in the best position to navigate ongoing changes and threats to your organization. And they are in the best position to bring clarity to *everything* because they are closest to the day-to-day lives of your employees.

Managers who give frequent and meaningful feedback have employees who are more likely to be engaged compared with managers who don't. The benefits of regular meaningful feedback for those who work remotely 80% to 100% of the time are even greater than for those who work on-site. The combination of autonomy and meaningful feedback is the magic formula that produces the greatest benefit. But poorly skilled managers fail to offer regular and useful feedback.

Frequency of Feedback Is Key to Engaging Remote Workers

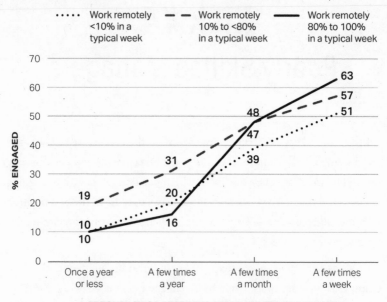

Source: Gallup Panel 2019 (pre-COVID-19)

The significance of this cannot be overstated: *Fully remote teams can substantially outperform on-site teams when they are managed effectively.*

Giving each employee meaningful feedback once a week is a basic requirement of a fully skilled manager.

But what does it mean to give regular meaningful feedback? First, you need to acknowledge that feedback is not just a manager-to-employee interaction. While a manager often initiates feedback, set the expectation that employees should also ask for feedback. In fact, the latter is often the least awkward approach.

Think of feedback as a busy two-way street.

The primary component of meaningful feedback is that it is tailored to the individual receiving it. This requires managers to have a basic knowledge and understanding of each individual, their goals and their strengths. Another component is timeliness. The problem with the traditional annual review is that feedback often comes months too late. Employees need ongoing conversations and continuous feedback because it is far more relevant and timely for the employee and the organization.

The intended outcome of meaningful feedback is inspiration, not just correction and advice. Poorly skilled managers don't get this. Having inspiring conversations builds engagement and trust between employees and managers, which leads to more transparent conversations.

Gallup's research shows a clear link between employee engagement and wellbeing, with managers serving as a conduit between the two. Engaged employees are more than twice as likely as actively disengaged employees to say they are very or somewhat comfortable discussing their wellbeing with their manager.

Giving each employee meaningful feedback once a week is a basic requirement of a fully skilled manager.

Yet managers who are poorly skilled at handling the complexities of today's workplace will inspire neither engagement nor wellbeing.

In all the risks to a net thriving culture that we identified — from mental health issues to the clarity of your purpose to policies, programs and perks — the evidence is clear: Designing an engaging workplace that is the foundation for thriving wellbeing and overall mental health is led by *the manager*.

Resilient Cultures in a Crisis

The four significant risks that can keep organizations from developing net thriving cultures — and other organizational threats — become magnified during societal and global crises such as economic crashes or pandemics.

This was especially true during the unprecedented crises that started in 2020. Employees' compounding uncertainty about COVID-19, a failing economy, joblessness, school closings, disrupted workplaces, social isolation and societal unrest made it the worst time most people have ever experienced. It took an exceptional amount of resilience for organizations and employees to thrive.

So how do you lead and inspire employees during a crisis or major disruption? The biggest differentiator is resilience.

A 2020 Gallup meta-analysis of 62,965 business units and teams, published in the peer-reviewed organizational science journal *Human Performance*, reported that favorable job attitudes have a stronger relationship to organizational outcomes in bad economic times than they do in normal or good times. The study looked at how key cultural attributes predicted profitability, productivity, customer perceptions of service and employee turnover from the mid-1990s through 2015 — which included two major economic recessions (2001-2002 and 2008-2009).

Even during good economic times, new threats keep coming. But net thriving and resilient cultures win in good times and bad. And compared with their peers, *net thriving, resilient cultures have superior performance.*

Gallup analysts dug deep into our databases to understand what leads to these types of outcomes over time. While we reported temporary changes in employee engagement during 2020, annually, we have found the percentage of engaged employees to be amazingly stable through various pandemics (e.g., West Nile virus, SARS, the Zika virus, bird flu), two major recessions and 9/11. Employee engagement changed *almost entirely in response to organizational practices,* such as top executive involvement, manager education, communication and accountability. During the COVID-19 pandemic, employee engagement at one point reached a new high.

The 2020 Gallup meta-analysis found that the relationship between engagement and performance *does* change during crises. In fact, during the past two major recessions, engagement has proven to be even *more* important than during good times.

Business units are at an increased advantage and more resilient — compared with their peers — if employee engagement is high. And they are at an increased disadvantage and less resilient if employee engagement is low.

Net thriving and resilient cultures win in good times and bad.

What Followers Need During a Crisis

Gallup's studies show that followers have four needs from their leaders, especially during crises. People look for these leadership traits as a signal that their life will be OK:

- Hope: Is there a clear plan for the future?

- Stability: Am I well-prepared to do my work?

- Trust: Does my manager keep me informed?

- Compassion: Does my organization care about my wellbeing?

Hope

In times of crisis, there are two directions human nature can take: fear, helplessness and victimization — or self-actualization and engagement.

Hope starts with leadership communicating a clear plan of action in response to the crisis.

In 2020, during the pandemic, the percentage of employees in Gallup's global database who strongly agreed that their leadership communicated a clear plan of action varied from four in 10 employees to nine in 10 employees. Organizations' effectiveness in this most basic of leadership requirements varied widely.

During a crisis, people need to see how they, and their work, fit into the bigger picture. They need to be able to see how their work affects your customers, mission and purpose, and the future of your organization. Human beings are amazingly resilient. When leaders have a clear way forward, there is a documented "rally effect."

One thing is clear. Employees look to leadership for a crisis management plan — and to give them confidence that there is a way forward.

Stability

As people adapt to disruptions, they return to basic needs. They need to feel prepared to do their work.

Across organizations in Gallup's 2020 global database, the percentage of employees who reported feeling strongly that they are well-prepared to do their work ranged from 30% to 80%.

During high-stress times, managers need to go back to the basics of clarifying expectations, reviewing material and equipment needs, and readjusting roles so that people can use their strengths in new ways.

During tough times, employees need managers who reset priorities, involve them in reestablishing their goals and constantly clarify their role relative to their coworkers' roles.

During a crisis, ongoing discussions about what resources employees need to get work done are vital to minimize stress and build resiliency.

Trust

In any crisis, when people are not getting timely information — no matter how negative — they start believing that someone is hiding something from them. Trust erodes, and self-preservation takes over. Stress, fear and anger emerge.

Supervisors or managers are the key conduits who are responsible for translating the organization's response to a crisis for each employee. And

In times of crisis, there are two directions human nature can take: fear, helplessness and victimization — or self-actualization and engagement.

only direct managers truly can know each employee's situation, keep them informed and adjust expectations accordingly.

The percentage of employees who strongly agree that their supervisor keeps them informed varied considerably across organizations during 2020 — from about 40% to 90%.

It takes highly engaged and talented managers to effectively keep employees updated during a crisis and to connect their team with other teams in the organization to maximize resiliency. Resilient and net thriving organizations have a plan for how they will continuously identify and develop the best managers. They know that a crisis requires a coach more than a boss.

Compassion

Before the novel coronavirus outbreak, work and life were more blended than ever before. Then suddenly in March 2020, millions of people were required to work from home — including kids being kept home from school. The blending of work and life became unbearable for many. It created unprecedented stress on mental health and wellbeing.

At the outset of the pandemic, less than half of U.S. employees (45%) strongly agreed that their organization cares about their overall wellbeing. Percentages were even lower in the U.K. (27%), France (26%) and Germany (32%). In Gallup's global database, the percentage of employees who strongly agree that their organization cares about their wellbeing varies from 30% to nearly 90% across organizations.

A key predictor of low worry and high confidence is whether each employee believes — and experiences — that their organization is looking out for their best interest. In organizations that care about employee wellbeing, managers are in tune with each individual's situation, and they can direct employees to personalized resources that improve their career, social, financial, physical and community wellbeing during the crisis.

Leading and inspiring employees through a crisis — and building organizational resilience — involves understanding fundamentals of human nature that are often overlooked.

PART 4:
Net Thriving Starts With
Career Engagement

The Largest Study of Its Kind

In the past 30 years, Gallup has interviewed 42.9 million employees on 5.1 million teams in more than 5,000 organizations in 212 countries.

This much is clear: The importance of improving the percentage of engaged workers cannot be overstated. Employee engagement is essential for a net thriving and resilient culture.

Global and U.S. Employee Engagement Trends

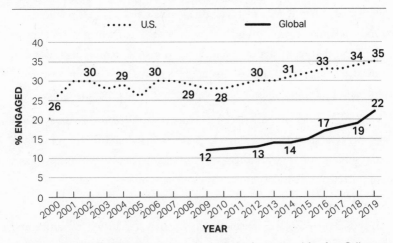

Percentages for global and U.S. engagement trends are calculated using annual data from Gallup random samples of the working population.

The percentage of engaged employees in both the U.S. and globally has gradually improved, particularly in the past decade. But workforce engagement isn't improving fast enough to fix performance and growing mental health challenges.

Gallup has studied organizations that achieved three or four times the global average of engaged employees. Even on Gallup's hardest-to-achieve engagement metric, the best organizations can exceed 70% engaged employees in their workforce. While every highly engaged organization has its own unique approach, the following common themes emerged:

1. Culture change was initiated by the CEO and board.

2. They transformed managers from boss to coach.

3. They practiced highly effective companywide communication.

4. They held managers accountable for engagement and performance.

Gallup's database has been the source for many research studies published in highly regarded scientific journals and business publications. One consistent theme from this database is that there is a core set of elements that consistently predict performance across organizations, industries and geographies — and across time during economic fluctuations, technological changes, pandemics and other disruptions.

This core set of workplace elements is captured in 12 survey items — the Gallup Q^{12}. Combined, these items quantify the employee engagement of a workforce — the involvement, enthusiasm and commitment of employees in any organization or geography.

Gallup analysts recently completed the 10th iteration of meta-analysis across 112,312 business units and teams in 54 industries and 96 countries. When comparing top- and bottom-quartile business units

Employee engagement is essential for a net thriving and resilient culture.

and teams, Gallup found that the top-quartile teams had substantially lower absenteeism, turnover, shrinkage, employee and patient accidents, and defects. They also had substantially higher customer engagement, productivity and sales. All of this accumulates into a 23% profitability advantage. The study also found that top-quartile business units had higher participation in company-sponsored activities and 66% higher rates of net thriving employees. (See Appendix 4 for a full technical report describing the details of this research.)

As we've noted, career wellbeing is the foundation for the other wellbeing elements. And employee engagement is the single biggest driver of career wellbeing.

Adopting Wellbeing Practices

Earlier we noted that many organizations have already adopted wellness programs and implemented benefits aimed at improving employee wellbeing. These efforts are well-intended, but the results range from mixed to ineffective.

For example, employees who use these programs are often already living healthy lifestyles or involved in their community. Employees who don't participate are more likely to be the least healthy or involved — those who need the programs most. People are complex, each with their own motivations. So how can you design an organizational system that works for all employees?

Gallup has found that adoption rates for wellbeing initiatives are substantially higher when people have great managers who engage them in their work first and establish trust. Here are some reasons why:

1. Engaged employees are more open and comfortable discussing broader wellbeing issues in their lives, and managers can quickly direct them toward positive solutions.

2. Engaged employees are less likely to question the intentions of wellbeing programs the company offers. *Are they just offering these things for show, or are they really trying to*

help me improve my life? It is difficult to get people excited about the organization's attempts to improve their wellbeing when their work is boring or miserable.

3. Engaged employees have strong relationships with others on their team. Research has shown that adoption of programs can be a product of social contagion among team members.

Your organization's best potential to create a net thriving culture starts when you master the elements of wellbeing most closely linked to *work*. This is because the work itself is a bridge to trust.

Today's employees have certain expectations of their employers. They expect clarity about their role; opportunities to use their strengths, develop a career, have a voice in decisions that affect their work; and to see their work contributing to an important mission and purpose. When organizations fail on any of these expectations, they lose credibility.

Simplifying Insights You Can Use Now

In the 13th century, the philosopher William of Ockham was credited with describing the "principle of parsimony" — commonly known as Occam's razor: Avoid excessive information to prove a theory if a simpler explanation fits the observation.

Albert Einstein, with his unparalleled brilliance, has often been attributed as saying that everything should be made as simple as possible, but not simpler.

At its best, science improves lives. But scientific findings that are too complex to be *applied* miss that mark. Gallup's goal is to synthesize our findings to identify conceptual and statistical redundancies to establish

> # It is difficult to get people excited about the organization's attempts to improve their wellbeing when their work is boring or miserable.

the most straightforward, useable insights — *as simple as possible, but not too simple.*

We have used this principle to identify the 12 engagement items from thousands of questions and to determine the five wellbeing elements.

Synthesizing even further, in the following sections, we'll highlight the five most important and highest priority engagement items:

- My expectations
- My strengths
- My development
- My opinions
- My mission or purpose

We'll describe why each of these engagement items is simultaneously essential to performance *and* wellbeing. And you can use our findings immediately to launch your journey to a net thriving culture.

My Expectations

Globally, one in two employees know what is expected of them at work.

That means half of employees worldwide are unsure about their roles. And even worse, they are stressed and anxious — even losing sleep — because they don't know what their boss wants from them. Half don't know if they're succeeding or failing. This damages their career wellbeing.

Those who report unclear expectations at work also report higher daily worry, stress, anxiety and loneliness.

On the other hand, those who say they have clear expectations at work are 26% more likely to be thriving in their overall lives.

The performance implications are substantial. By increasing the ratio of employees who know what's expected of them from one in two to eight in 10, organizations can realize a 22% reduction in turnover, a 29% reduction in safety incidents and a 10% increase in productivity.

Clear expectations are an employee's most fundamental need.

Without them, no corporate program, initiative or culture can succeed. However, many veteran leaders and established companies don't get this right. Less than half of employees (43%) strongly agree that they have a clear job description, and even fewer (41%) strongly agree that their job description aligns with the work they do.

Those who report unclear expectations at work also report higher daily worry, stress, anxiety and loneliness.

The employees who strongly agree that their job description aligns with the work they do are 2.5 times more likely than other employees to be engaged. But the greatest pitfall of the first engagement item is that managers assume there's a simple solution: "If people don't know what's expected, I'll just tell them."

Getting employees to understand *what's expected* requires much more than telling them what to do. Employees need to understand the fundamentals of their work, which include — but are not limited to — their job description.

In today's highly matrixed workplace, employees are often on multiple teams with various team leaders who have many different priorities. While these employees may report high levels of collaboration and get along with their colleagues, they still don't know what to do first. This creates anxiety and stress.

Even worse, managers are typically less clear about expectations than their employees are.

In many cases, employees and their managers are being held accountable for work that may or may not correspond with the work they're being evaluated on. For this reason, one of the most important roles in management is to provide meaningful feedback *multiple times a week* — once a week at a minimum — through check-ins, quick connects and developmental conversations. Central to these meetings is discussing *goals*.

Use these science-based insights as guidance for giving your employees clear expectations:

- **Set clear goals.** A meta-analysis of 74 studies published in *Journal of Management* found that clear, less ambiguous goals for an individual's role were related to increased productivity. Another meta-analysis of 49 studies published in *Journal of Applied Psychology* found that specific and difficult goals were associated with higher performance. Even moderately difficult goals were associated with higher performance as long as they were not ambiguous.

- **Provide adequate resources.** A meta-analysis published in *Journal of Vocational Behavior* found that difficult goals can cause burnout if employees don't have the supporting resources to do the work.

- **Lead collaborative goal setting.** Gallup has found that just 30% of employees strongly agree that their manager involves them in setting their goals at work. But those who do strongly agree are 3.1 times more likely than other employees to be engaged.

- **Nurture collective intelligence.** Numerous studies show the importance of individuals knowing how their roles relate to their teammates' roles. Team members gain "tacit knowledge" or "shared cognition" as they work together over time. Individuals progressively get better at anticipating how their team members respond in various situations. They also can get better over time at retaining this information and applying it to new situations.

"Clear expectations" may sound basic, but when you apply them consistently, they are deeply gratifying to employees. When a manager and employee set goals and clarify expectations together, it is motivating. It spurs ownership, action, creativity and innovation — because everybody determines the goal.

My Strengths

One in three employees around the world strongly agree that they have the opportunity to do what they do best every day.

These employees are using their natural talents and strengths at work on a consistent basis. Those who are not doing what they do best report higher rates of boredom in their daily lives. They have lower energy throughout the day and are more likely to be struggling or suffering in their overall lives.

A Gallup study tracked employees during their workday and asked them to report what they were feeling at specific moments. Employees who, prior to the study, reported that they had an opportunity to do what they do best also reported much higher energy in those moments than other employees did. This has both wellbeing and performance implications.

When managers position people to use their natural talents and strengths, they get better results.

Energy During Moments of the Day

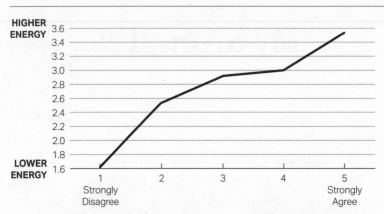

AT WORK, I HAVE THE OPPORTUNITY TO DO WHAT I DO BEST EVERY DAY.

Note: Median individual summaries of approximately 750 momentary ratings across 152 participants during work time. For further description of the methods used, see Harter & Stone (2012).

Use these science-based insights as guidance for giving your employees the opportunity to do what they do best:

- **Build a scientific "job fit" system.** Matching the right person with the right job is a complicated responsibility. A meta-analysis of 172 studies published in *Personnel Psychology* found "job fit" — the match of job knowledge, skills and abilities to perform the job requirements — to be highly related to job attitudes, performance and wellbeing. Another review across 100 years of selection research by Gallup Senior Scientist Frank Schmidt and his colleagues found that scientific methods of selection, based on innate tendencies, substantially improve performance. Organizations that miss this first step face an uphill battle.

136

- **Identify and embrace unique strengths within roles.** No matter how good your selection system is, the people you hire in any role are likely to have considerable variation in their strengths — their innate ways of relating, influencing, executing and strategic thinking. This variance exists across all demographic categories such as race, gender and age. Gallup studies indicate that an individual's strengths are not likely to change substantially over the course of 10 years or more. Other studies of heritability support this finding, over even longer time spans. So the best way to set your employees up for success is to identify and develop the strengths they already have.

- **Give employees challenging assignments that align with their natural abilities.** Gallup conducted a "day reconstruction" study, asking 8,115 participants to relive their previous workday — how much time they spent doing various activities and how they felt during those activities. The single best predictor of high engagement and low disengagement was the amount of time employees said they were so absorbed in what they were doing that time

When managers position people to use their natural talents and strengths, they get better results.

passed quickly — what Gallup Senior Scientist Emeritus Mihaly Csikszentmihalyi calls a state of "flow." To determine each employee's natural talents and strengths, during developmental conversations, great managers ask employees to describe the times when they experience flow.

As we'll discuss in Part 5, the practice of identifying and applying strengths provides a shortcut to improving wellbeing for each person.

My Development

For an employee to feel that their organization cares about their wellbeing, they first need to have someone at work who cares about them as a person.

The ultimate caring is investing in someone's future — their professional and personal growth. In fact, Gallup research shows that development is strongly linked to employees feeling that their organization values their overall wellbeing.

Globally, just three in 10 employees strongly agree that someone at work encourages their development.

Of the engagement items, the development item is the most important one to get right when building a net thriving culture.

When people are not growing and developing, their thinking becomes narrower and more self-serving — *What's in it for me?* — rather than company-focused — *How can our team collaborate with other teams to do what's best for our customers?*

Development starts at the top. The problem is, Gallup data show that only one in three managers strongly agree that someone at work encourages *their* development, despite major investments in their training. And Gallup finds that as tenure increases, the opportunity to learn and grow decreases.

It's not that organizations haven't tried to fix the problem. The issue has become so serious that HR departments have inflated employees' titles and job levels to make them *feel* like they're developing.

Two-thirds of people who change jobs change companies, rather than find new jobs with their current employer. And the top reason people change companies is lack of career development. It is a leadership mistake not to create a path of clear potential for employees inside their own company.

Are your managers "talent hoarders" or "star makers"? The answer says a lot about your employment brand because what happens inside your organization will spread through social media.

A Gallup study during the recession following the 2008 financial crash found that employees who said someone at work *encourages their development* had more positive views of their standard of living; they could see a more positive future.

For an employee's experiencing self, development makes life more interesting and more fun. *Interesting work* is the difference between burnout and flow.

In contrast, doing work that feels the same — over and over, year after year — grinds the spirit out of people. The best employees often quit their jobs because no one talked with them about their future.

For an employee's remembering self, there's a deep satisfaction when they reflect on how far they've come. Everyone wants to feel like they're making progress — to be healthier, to be a better parent, to become more financially secure, and to increase their skills and competencies. When employees reflect on their lives, it's their periods of growth — often very challenging — that give them the deepest sense of satisfaction.

Doing work that feels the same — over and over, year after year — grinds the spirit out of people.

Use these science-based insights as guidance for giving your employees exceptional development experiences:

- **Design a system for mentoring.** A meta-analysis of 166 studies found that individuals with mentors had substantially higher performance, intentions to stay with their organization, cooperation with coworkers, positive attitudes toward their career, overall motivation and better health practices. Also, a series of studies has shown that goal alignment between the individual and mentor substantially strengthens career wellbeing. So, be sure to find the right fit between mentors and mentees.

- **Focus on goals.** A meta-analysis of 607 studies found that regular feedback improves performance — but the impact depends on the type of feedback. A 60-year review of goal-setting research found that adding goals to developmental feedback substantially improves performance. When setting goals, identify key experiences for every role, such as stretch assignments, cross-functional collaboration and mentoring.

- **Use validated manager training.** Gallup has found that managers who receive training that builds their skills to use strengths to engage employees has 2.5 times the impact on their team's engagement compared with a control group that didn't receive the same advanced training.

- **Watch out for manager burnout.** While managers play the greatest role in creating a net thriving culture, they have higher burnout and stress than those they manage. Form peer groups where managers can share wellbeing success strategies.

My Opinions

Feeling like your opinions matter is closely tied to respect. There can be no culture of respect in the absence of dialogue between managers and employees. And yet globally, only one in four employees strongly agree that their opinions count at work.

Two-thirds of employees who think their opinions count are thriving in their overall lives.

Deliberately seeking out employee opinions is especially important with remote workers. These employees can experience isolation, loneliness and disengagement — it's easy to leave them out of the loop.

Not feeling like their opinions count is a key factor in employee burnout. Consider an employee's frustration as they repeatedly communicate: *This isn't working!* Employees feel powerless when they don't think anyone hears them. As a result, their work and wellbeing both suffer.

When leaders solicit and use their followers' opinions, it creates buy-in. Employees feel like, "I built this."

The best managers use their team as the key resource for better decision-making. They encourage dialogue and debate and create a team culture of problem-solving.

Use these science-based insights as guidance for giving your employees opportunities to make their opinions count:

- **Seek employee input.** A meta-analysis of 88 studies found that people in cultures where managers seek input from employees had fewer reports of physical health symptoms and emotional distress.

- **Empower your employees — they'll live longer.** The Whitehall studies, which included 17,530 British civil servants in one study and 10,314 in another, were originally led by Sir Michael Marmot, who aimed to longitudinally study the social determinants of health. Many of the findings are discussed in research papers and Marmot's book *The Status Syndrome.* The primary finding was that people with less perceived control had higher rates of coronary heart disease and higher mortality rates — and the workplace was found to be an important contributing factor.

Not feeling like their opinions count is a key factor in employee burnout.

My Mission or Purpose

More than nine in 10 people say they have a purpose that makes their life important.

But globally, just one in three employees strongly agree that the mission or purpose of their organization makes them feel their job is important.

While millennials and Generation Z in particular demand purpose-driven, mission-oriented work, all generations rate an organization's purpose as a key factor when looking for a job.

An employee's experiencing self goes to work every day not just because of a paycheck, but because their work matters. As we highlighted earlier, feeling connected to a mission or purpose is a requirement for resiliency during hard times.

An employee's remembering self may, in middle age, begin to question what they have truly contributed to the world. When employees in any job near retirement, they might ask, "What was all that for?"

If a job were just a job, it really wouldn't matter where someone worked. Employees want meaning in what they do every day. For reasons that transcend the physical needs fulfilled by earning a living, people look for their contribution to a higher purpose. Employees want to believe in what their employer does. As humans, they need to belong to something, whether it's their company, community, sports team, local theater troupe, children's museum or church.

Every company has a mission statement, but *it's the manager who makes work meaningful.*

The best managers deepen a sense of purpose by clarifying the organization's mission, helping employees see their role in it and giving employees opportunities to talk about it.

Use these science-based insights as guidance for making your organization's mission and purpose integral to each employee's work and wellbeing:

- **Make your mission or purpose clear and concise so every employee can relate it to the work they do every day.**
  A clear purpose drives resiliency, wellbeing and financial outcomes. A recent study of 429 companies examined the relationship between employee perceptions of purpose and financial outcomes for publicly traded companies. On its own, purpose did not explain differences in financial outcomes without clear communication from senior management. So make sure to be transparent about what your organization stands for.

- **Get out in front of burnout.** Even if your organization has a well-articulated mission or purpose that every employee can remember, constantly changing priorities with no vision, rhyme or reason and bad managers will create anxiety for your employees. This is a recipe for stress, anger and eventually burnout. Remember that your employees need more than just a clear mission statement; they need a great manager.

Every company has a mission statement, but it's the manager who makes work meaningful.

PART 5:
The Fastest Road to
Net Thriving:
Play to Strengths

Strengths Make Wellbeing Work

"To succeed in this new world, we will have to learn, first, who we are. Few people, even highly successful people, can answer the questions, 'Do you know what you're good at?' 'Do you know what you need to learn so that you get the full benefit of your strengths?' Few have even asked themselves these questions."

— Peter Drucker (1909-2005)

You can achieve net thriving without taking extreme measures or fundamentally changing who you are:

- You don't need to be an athlete to be healthy — you only need a moderate amount of physical activity every day.

- You don't need to be a multimillionaire to feel financially secure — the key is to live within your means.

- And you don't need to make 10 new friends to improve your social life — you just need relationships that give you energy.

Improving wellbeing requires changing habits. So how do you make it easier for people to do things that are best for them in the long term? The key is to identify your employees' unique strengths and aim them toward high wellbeing.

Managers should have conversations with their employees about wellbeing, but only when you have built a foundation of trust. Wellbeing conversations without that personal connection can be a minefield. This is why starting wellbeing discussions with an employee's strengths is so effective. These discussions:

- focus on the individual's positive contributions

- don't include awkward criticism that puts them on the defense

- identify what makes them unique

- establish a common language for strengths-based development that contributes to net thriving

When you can identify the specific strengths of an employee, you will know what that employee finds interesting, engaging, important and valuable. This empowers you to have meaningful conversations and match wellbeing activities with that individual's interests.

Led by the lifetime work of Dr. Don Clifton, Gallup has studied human potential through strengths for five decades and discovered 34 talent themes, which we've deployed through the CliftonStrengths assessment. See Appendix 1 for insights and action items for the five wellbeing elements for each of the 34 CliftonStrengths themes. To discover your own strengths, use the unique access code in the packet in the back of the book to take the CliftonStrengths assessment yourself.

Combining strengths and wellbeing at work is potentially the most transformational treatment yet in the urgent pursuit of resiliency, mental health and ultimately, net thriving.

You can achieve net thriving

without taking extreme measures or

fundamentally changing who you are.

APPENDIXES

Appendix 1:
Strengths Insights and Action Items for the Five Wellbeing Elements

---

Each of your employees is unique. Knowing your employees' strengths is the first step to having the most individualized, positive and effective wellbeing conversations with them.

Once you know your employees' strengths profiles, find their top CliftonStrengths in this appendix. Then use the insights and action items for the five wellbeing elements — specific to each strength — as part of your wellbeing discussions. Focusing on strengths is the best and fastest way to start your employees on a wellbeing journey toward a thriving life.

ACHIEVER

People exceptionally talented in the Achiever theme work hard and possess a great deal of stamina. They take immense satisfaction in being busy and productive.

- **Career:** Help this person excel by collaborating with them to establish a development plan that includes metrics to track their progress. When projects come along that align with their plan, ask if they would like to run them.

- **Social:** This person may not make time for valuable relationships when they are focused on a project. When possible, pair them with colleagues they like and with whom they can be productive.

- **Financial:** This person may be struggling with the financial goals they're working toward. Help them set up a system — using a software program or smartphone app — to track their progress.

- **Physical:** This person may or may not have their Achiever theme aimed at their physical wellbeing. Ask them about their goals, including exercise, weight loss, daily steps, nutrition and sleep. Coach them to celebrate increments of achievement along the way to their big goals.

- **Community:** Discover this person's passions, and encourage them to find community organizations where they can use their passion to contribute, serve and be productive.

ACTIVATOR

People exceptionally talented in the Activator theme can make things happen by turning thoughts into action. They want to do things now, rather than simply talk about them.

- **Career:** When a project needs a lift, ask this person to jump-start it. Let them know that they have natural talent to drive people toward action.

- **Social:** When you need someone to bring people together around a common goal or activity, look to this person to rally everyone. They will find it invigorating to engage in the initial phase of planning and urge others to participate.

- **Financial:** This person may strive toward financial goals but lose momentum along the way. To keep them focused on the finish line, coach them to identify an accountability partner or to use a tool that tracks their financial progress.

- **Physical:** When the team needs a boost of energy, ask this person to get everyone up and moving around. Whether it is activating people to stretch over a Zoom call or take a walk, their energy can boost the physical and emotional wellbeing of the group.

- **Community:** During your next check-in, ask this person what community events or activities energize them. For example — depending on their passion — they might start an initiative to feed the hungry, buy school supplies for underserved students or begin a mentoring program for at-risk youth.

ADAPTABILITY

People exceptionally talented in the Adaptability theme prefer to go with the flow. They tend to be "now" people who take things as they come and discover the future one day at a time.

- **Career:** This person is inclined to remain cool, calm and collected during times of organizational change or shifts in team priorities. When your team is going through changes, ask them to say a few words at your team meeting. Their demeanor can ease anxiety and uncertainty.

- **Social:** When working with other employees to plan companywide events, this person can be the calm in the storm. They help anxious colleagues see that no matter what, they will make it work and that the event will be a success.

- **Financial:** This person may struggle to save for major life expenses, such as buying a home or planning for retirement. They live in the moment. A financial planner could serve as a complementary partner to help them make long-term plans as well as fun shorter-term goals for entertainment and family vacations.

- **Physical:** Following a rigorous and structured workout plan probably won't work for this person. They are more likely to stick to a program when they are part of a group that expects them to show up and understands that there may be days when they feel like doing something different.

- **Community:** Remember that this person loves to be "in the moment" and is less inclined to plan ahead. They will find joy in reviewing the calendar of events in their local community and then choosing one at the last minute.

ANALYTICAL

People exceptionally talented in the Analytical theme search for reasons and causes. They have the ability to think about all of the factors that might affect a situation.

- **Career:** This person loves details. Have them serve as a thought partner for colleagues by examining all possibilities in the data and resources presented in any initiative. They will ensure that the team has a well-thought-out strategy before moving forward.

- **Social:** A game or conversation that involves strategy and insight allows this person to connect with colleagues, friends and family while finding joy in facts, knowledge and problem-solving.

- **Financial:** This person thrives when they discover patterns in data. Coach them to apply their skills to analyzing their own financial situation and progress toward short- and long-term goals.

- **Physical:** This person likes to study the science behind their fitness and health goals to understand how life choices affect their outcomes. Ask them how they are applying the latest findings and to share their discoveries with the team.

- **Community:** This person can use their ability to analyze data to demonstrate whether or not a community project works and how to make it better.

ARRANGER

People exceptionally talented in the Arranger theme can organize, but they also have a flexibility that complements this ability. They like to determine how all of the pieces and resources can be arranged for maximum productivity.

- **Career:** This person is a conductor. They thrive when there are a lot of moving pieces that need to fit together. Put them in charge of hard and complex assignments.

- **Social:** This person loves to plan big celebrations. Ask them to coordinate major events inside and outside of the organization.

- **Financial:** Help this person use their Arranger talent to consider all the moving parts of their finances that work together to achieve their short- and long-term goals.

- **Physical:** Rather than following a highly dedicated routine, this person will draw the most energy from having a variety of healthy choices, such as eating more vegetables, improving sleep habits, walking the kids to school, bike riding to meet friends or going to the gym.

- **Community:** This person should consider being a leader in a local nonprofit. They should also be seen as a leader of their organization's volunteer efforts because they will match the right people with the right purpose.

BELIEF

People exceptionally talented in the Belief theme have certain core values that are unchanging. Out of these values emerges a defined purpose for their lives.

- **Career:** Recognize that this person has a core set of values that defines their life. Help them connect the dots between their daily work and the organization's larger mission and contribution to society.

- **Social:** Managers should know that this person thrives in relationships with people who share their strong sense of belief and their commitment to a clear set of chosen values. Coach them to seek out ways to connect with those people.

- **Financial:** This person will be motivated to create an investment strategy that aligns with their values and beliefs.

- **Physical:** Coach this person to understand how physical and mental health connect to living their mission. Good rest, nutrition and exercise allow them to be at their best so they can continue to make a difference in the lives of their family and community.

- **Community:** This person thrives when getting their team behind a cause they believe in. Whether they're rallying people to support a food drive, run in a 5K race for a charity or serve the homeless, their ability to speak with passion about what is most meaningful to them can get people to support their cause.

COMMAND

People exceptionally talented in the Command theme have presence. They can take control of a situation and make decisions.

- **Career:** As a natural leader, this person thrives on taking charge and helping the team make progress to achieve their priorities. Managers can rely on their strong presence to bring clarity and make hard decisions.

- **Social:** Sometimes this person can come on strong. When they're trying to connect with others, coach them to ease up on their Command to find common ground. Advise them that doing so will allow others to see their more compassionate side, thereby potentially creating more friendships.

- **Financial:** This person thrives on taking the lead and may enjoy managing their own finances or working with a financial adviser who is also direct and who "calls it like they see it."

- **Physical:** This person can inspire and motivate others to achieve their fitness goals. For instance, they could form a local intramural team and serve as the captain; or in the workplace, they can take the lead on creating a wellbeing committee.

- **Community:** This person's strong presence and take-charge attitude can rally people to support a cause. They will thrive when you ask them to use their Command talents for hard assignments, such as raising funds for a community organization.

COMMUNICATION

People exceptionally talented in the Communication theme generally find it easy to put their thoughts into words. They are good conversationalists and presenters.

- **Career:** This person takes great satisfaction from communicating with others. They are often natural presenters and speakers. Their wellbeing will soar when their storytelling talent is used to motivate teams.

- **Social:** During team huddles or quarterly events, build in time for this person to share the team's successes. They will likely have an engaging way of delivering recognition, which will attract people to them.

- **Financial:** This person processes their thoughts out loud, so connect them with someone they trust to talk through their vision and strategies for their financial future.

- **Physical:** This person gets energy from conversing with others, so coach them to exercise with a friend. Hiking, biking or walking are some ways that they could achieve the benefits of exercise and self-expression with someone else.

- **Community:** Recognize that this person has a natural way of expressing their thoughts and emotions through spoken words. Have them consider a cause that is close to their heart that could use a powerful voice to amplify its message and drive others toward action.

COMPETITION

People exceptionally talented in the Competition theme measure their progress against the performance of others. They strive to win first place and revel in contests.

- **Career:** This person thrives when measuring their accomplishments against others. They will love leading the charge against the company's competitors.

- **Social:** Help this person find a group of like-minded individuals who love to compete and win. This can give them a healthy outlet to release their competitive drive.

- **Financial:** Gamification and accountability partners will inspire this person to reach their financial goals. Help them find smartphone apps that allow them to accrue points for each financial milestone they reach, or encourage them to share their financial goals with a trusted partner.

- **Physical:** First place is the *only* place for this person. Activities with a leaderboard will be the driving force that keeps them motivated. They may prefer to join a top-ranked intramural sports team they can help lead to victory.

- **Community:** Ask this person about their hobbies and personal interests. They can inject a sense of confidence and a winning attitude for those who need a boost, whether it is for a nonprofit, charity or any volunteer organization.

CONNECTEDNESS

People exceptionally talented in the Connectedness theme have faith in the links among all things. They believe there are few coincidences and that almost every event has meaning.

- **Career:** Pull in this person to help connect everyone to the team's goals. They can help their colleagues see how all the team's work-related tasks fit together.

- **Social:** This person can bring calm during times of chaos and uncertainty because they see how the whole is greater than the sum of its parts. They can help friends, family and colleagues make peace with the past and have faith in what is to come.

- **Financial:** If this person is making a spending or investment decision, coach them to see that even the tiniest choice is connected to the larger whole. They will understand that no decisions exist in isolation.

- **Physical:** This person feels they are "at one" with nature and humanity. Encourage them to spend time outdoors hiking or running — this will energize them. Meditation and yoga can connect them to their inner self and the world around them.

- **Community:** When the world is suffering, this person will feel a heightened sense of duty to bring people together and help them to see that everything happens for a reason. Remind them that their ability to unite generates more commitment to serious societal issues.

CONSISTENCY

People exceptionally talented in the Consistency theme are keenly aware of the need to treat people the same. They crave stable routines and clear rules and procedures that everyone can follow.

- **Career:** When the team faces serious uncertainty, ask this person to help establish team standards. They will provide stability, fairness and confidence.

- **Social:** This person holds everyone to the same standards and procedures, creating fairness and equity. They will build relationships leading a youth group or sports team, where these guidelines create a more harmonious team.

- **Financial:** The need to establish rules is key to this person's financial wellbeing. Due to their consistent financial practices, any changes to their compensation system will create disruption. If this happens, refer them to a benefits representative who can help them.

- **Physical:** This person enjoys structure and predictability. They will thrive creating a consistent fitness and health routine that they can control. Sticking to a clear plan raises their wellbeing.

- **Community:** Getting involved in causes and nonprofits that this person can improve by introducing rules and standards greatly contributes both to the cause and to their own wellbeing.

CONTEXT

People exceptionally talented in the Context theme enjoy thinking about the past. They understand the present by researching its history.

- **Career:** This person has a deep interest in history. They look back to make sense of today. Count on them when the team needs background information or case studies to help see the way forward.

- **Social:** Recognize that this person finds enjoyment in understanding the past. A weekend spent antiquing or visiting museums with others will energize them. They are the much-appreciated historian for friends and family.

- **Financial:** This person can take the long view on how investments have performed over time, from stocks to real estate to the extraordinary power of compounding interest. Coach them to use this talent to see where spending and investing have worked or gone wrong in the past.

- **Physical:** This person studies the history of the most effective diets and workout programs — which have been proven to work — rather than following each new fad. This helps them pick the right program.

- **Community:** This person will love volunteering at their local historical society where they can work alongside other history buffs to share the unique narrative of their community with residents. They will also thrive when involved in nonprofits with rich, long histories.

DELIBERATIVE

People exceptionally talented in the Deliberative theme are best described by the serious care they take in making decisions or choices. They anticipate obstacles.

- **Career:** This person brings a thoughtful approach to decision-making. They can slow down impulsive decisions to take time to get the facts, which is an asset to any workplace team.

- **Social:** This person takes time to build relationships. They will thrive when you partner them with colleagues they already trust. They do not offer praise easily — remind them that giving recognition is important.

- **Financial:** This person is the opposite of an impulse buyer. They are a "think long and hard" buyer. They will thrive with a financial adviser who understands their need for extra time to consider investment strategies.

- **Physical:** This person will appreciate talking to an expert to identify the best options for stress relief, nutrition and exercise. They won't have confidence in a plan — and won't start or continue it — unless they have thoroughly studied and vetted it.

- **Community:** This person's intentional approach to problem-solving can help local charities and nonprofits carefully think through their long-term strategic plan.

DEVELOPER

People exceptionally talented in the Developer theme recognize and cultivate the potential in others. They spot the signs of each small improvement and derive satisfaction from evidence of progress.

- **Career:** This person has a natural talent for developing people. Encourage them to inspire high-potential employees.

- **Social:** Encourage this person to offer advice and guidance to friends and family. They have a gift for seeing capacity for growth. They draw enormous energy from seeing others develop.

- **Financial:** Given their focus on others, this person may not be interested in their own financial wellbeing goals. Encourage them to build a relationship with a professional who can help them see how managing their money well allows them to give more to others.

- **Physical:** As this person establishes better exercise, nutrition and sleep habits, encourage them to share their knowledge and experience with others. They will enjoy inspiring others' progress.

- **Community:** As an expert developer, this person can play a key role in nearly any nonprofit or charity where they can help others grow. They can see the overall potential of the organization and its leaders.

DISCIPLINE

People exceptionally talented in the Discipline theme enjoy routine and structure. Their world is best described by the order they create.

- **Career:** This person is good at building structure for themselves and the group. They will thrive when you put them in roles where they can create order out of chaos.

- **Social:** This person thrives in the planning and perfectionism of putting on any social gathering or event. Help them find activities to use this strength — it will attract others to them.

- **Financial:** This person has a set budget for groceries, utilities, housing, entertainment and investments. Coach them to use financial planning applications so they can track their expenses in one place.

- **Physical:** Sticking to a routine is key to this person's overall wellbeing. They have a set time of day for meals, exercise and rest. Realize that a schedule change will be disruptive to them and affect their wellbeing.

- **Community:** This person will thrive when bringing systems and order to a local community organization.

EMPATHY

People exceptionally talented in the Empathy theme can sense other people's feelings by imagining themselves in others' lives or situations.

- **Career:** This person has a gift — to feel what their colleagues are feeling. Think of them as mind readers. They will thrive when you seek their advice and feedback on the mood of individuals and the team.

- **Social:** Friends and family value how much this person understands them. However, because of their high Empathy, they might not pay attention to their own needs. Encourage them to spend time with people who give them positive energy.

- **Financial:** Since this person is deeply other-oriented, coach them to connect their investing to helping the people they care most about.

- **Physical:** This person tends to carry the burden of the emotions and problems of others. Help them find a release through exercise, meditation or other activities.

- **Community:** Coach this person to use their understanding of other people's concerns to work through hard issues in their community.

FOCUS

People exceptionally talented in the Focus theme can take a direction, follow through and make the corrections necessary to stay on track. They prioritize, then act.

- **Career:** When the team veers off track during a project, this person will thrive when you rely on them to refocus the group. As a result, they can help the team prioritize and hit deadlines.

- **Social:** This person can become so fixated on personal and professional goals that they lose sight of their relationships. Coach them to pay attention to who they are with in each moment.

- **Financial:** Encourage this person to focus on a long-term financial plan. Teach them what goals to aim at within the plan — and they will stick to it.

- **Physical:** It is likely that this person has a particular outcome they would like to achieve. It could be losing weight, reducing stress, improving sleep or lowering their glucose. They will do best when they focus on one goal.

- **Community:** This person will make the most impact in their community and on people's lives when they contribute to one thing rather than several. They will thrive when they can concentrate on a single cause.

FUTURISTIC

People exceptionally talented in the Futuristic theme are inspired by the future and what could be. They energize others with their visions of the future.

- **Career:** This person thrives when living in the future. Ask them to connect the task at hand to where it all leads. They will energize the team and customers by sharing their vision of the future.

- **Social:** This person thrives socially when they are in stimulating conversations with others about the future. Urge them to seek out similarly future-thinking friends and associates.

- **Financial:** This individual can be easily coached to consider how short-term money decisions affect long-term financial security.

- **Physical:** Encourage this person to take steps *today* to achieve a health goal. They are most likely to be successful if what they do today is connected to 20 years from now.

- **Community:** This person brings energy to any charity or nonprofit because they love seeing a better future for the community. Their vision attracts and inspires more volunteers and donations.

HARMONY

People exceptionally talented in the Harmony theme look for consensus. They don't enjoy conflict; rather, they seek areas of agreement.

- **Career:** This person has an instinctive ability to find common ground. Talk to them about the last time they brought peace to a situation at work by moving from conflict to agreement. They will soar when you ask them to help the team collaborate.

- **Social:** This person will thrive in groups that agree on basic issues and values. Social conflict is stressful for them. Coach them to spend time with people who have similar views.

- **Financial:** This person is likely to feel stress when they receive multiple opinions on important decisions they face. Their Harmony is best served when they follow the recommendations of *one* financial expert versus many.

- **Physical:** This person needs to be intentional about how they process stress from conflict. Discover with them what method works best to release stress and maintain harmony. Then coach them to do it every day.

- **Community:** Encourage this person to find community organizations that align with their values versus ones that center around issues and conflict. They will experience their highest wellbeing in service roles instead of political or special interest groups.

IDEATION

People exceptionally talented in the Ideation theme are fascinated by ideas. They are able to find connections between seemingly disparate phenomena.

- **Career:** This person loves ideas and brainstorming about anything. They experience flow — being so absorbed that time passes quickly — when you create an environment that allows them to think freely to get to a breakthrough. Their wellbeing will hit new highs and make an extraordinary contribution to your teams and customers.

- **Social:** This person will thrive in the presence of others with high Ideation. They are inspired by others' innovation — not unlike great jazz musicians. Help them find environments that stimulate high creativity and innovation, such as conferences and festivals.

- **Financial:** This person's wellbeing will be highest when their imagination is not bogged down by financial worries. Carefully coach them to live within their means. Better yet, help them find a financial adviser who also leads with Ideation.

- **Physical:** Encourage this person to find an exercise partner they can talk and ideate with. Or if they are going to exercise by themselves, suggest that they also use the time to ponder on a specific subject that is important to them.

- **Community:** This person's best day is when they are asked to come up with a really big idea. They will thrive when given a hard innovation challenge. For instance, they might come up with a grand inspiration to create a river walk — one that would attract visitors and investors and save the vibrancy of a downtown area.

INCLUDER

People exceptionally talented in the Includer theme accept others. They show awareness of those who feel left out and make an effort to include them.

- **Career:** This person is very egalitarian. They want everyone at work to feel accepted. Includers soar when no one is left out. The world's workplace needs Includers more than ever.

- **Social:** This person is gifted at making people feel welcome and included. This gift attracts people to them.

- **Financial:** This person will welcome people — to a fault — and invite too many to their dinners or gatherings, which can get very expensive. Coach them on the importance of not overdoing it.

- **Physical:** This person loves to involve people in every aspect of life. Coach them to use their Includer strength when arranging group exercise activities that everybody can participate in.

- **Community:** This person would be great at bringing together a town hall or community event where a broad mix of people can share their opinions and concerns. They will thrive when asked to do this.

INDIVIDUALIZATION

People exceptionally talented in the Individualization theme are intrigued with the unique qualities of each person. They have a gift for figuring out how different people can work together productively.

- **Career:** As someone who understands how each individual is different, this person will soar when you ask them who the best person for a job is.

- **Social:** Friends and family appreciate how well this person pays attention to their hobbies and interests and gives them gifts that are personal. In the workplace, they can help identify the best way to recognize a specific team member's achievements.

- **Financial:** A one-size-fits-all approach to this person's finances will likely frustrate them. They do best with financial advisers who understand their individual needs and goals.

- **Physical:** This person is inclined to appreciate a customized approach to their health and wellness. They will thrive when a nutritionist or personal trainer designs a program for their specific goals.

- **Community:** Who is the right person to run the fundraiser? Who is the right person to run the annual fair, the yearly membership drive or the reception for the children's museum? This person will know and will thrive when you ask them.

INPUT

People exceptionally talented in the Input theme have a need to collect and archive. They may accumulate information, ideas, artifacts or even relationships.

- **Career:** This person thrives when providing information to others. They can serve as a formal or informal subject matter expert in the company and be a valuable resource to any team.

- **Social:** People close to this person appreciate their ability to share useful knowledge. Friends and family can look to them for advice on anything from a good book to a restaurant to a TV series. They love when you seek their feedback.

- **Financial:** This person loves collecting and sharing information. They will thrive when asked to study investment options for their colleagues and to report their discoveries to the group.

- **Physical:** This person will enjoy gathering the latest research on ways to improve mental and physical wellbeing in general — and will revel in sharing their findings with others.

- **Community:** Encourage this person to serve as a board member or adviser in the community, where their love for gathering and sharing information supports the goals of the organization.

INTELLECTION

People exceptionally talented in the Intellection theme are characterized by their intellectual activity. They are introspective and appreciate intellectual discussions.

- **Career:** Look for opportunities to give this person the freedom to reflect and to use their full intellectual ability. They will appreciate the time to "noodle" on new information, people or processes before putting ideas and opinions together on how to proceed.

- **Social:** Due to their need for solitude and reflection, this person may prefer reading a book or watching a documentary alone. When they do engage with friends and family, they may appreciate book clubs or Sundays at the museum.

- **Financial:** This person will enjoy a thorough education on the stock market or on the best methods for paying off debt. They will thrive exploring books or websites that deepen their knowledge, or you might suggest that they find a podcast hosted by a prominent financial expert.

- **Physical:** Some activities that might appeal to this person are hikes in nature, meditation or swimming laps in a pool because they like to have time to think. Or they might enjoy making sure they get plenty of rest to boost their immune system to stay mentally sharp.

- **Community:** This person's appreciation for intellectual conversation and debate can bring thought-provoking questions to the forefront and get others to think differently and take action. They may enjoy community associations where they can engage in meaningful discussions that make a real impact.

LEARNER

People exceptionally talented in the Learner theme have a great desire to learn and want to continuously improve. The process of learning, rather than the outcome, excites them.

- **Career:** This person appreciates continual opportunities for learning and development. Ask them what they are most interested in learning about at work, and then partner them with an expert from the organization. Encourage them to host a presentation for the team to share their new knowledge.

- **Social:** This person's natural curiosity and quest for knowledge is evident in new classes they enroll in or new languages they learn. They may enjoy asking a friend to join them so they both can share in the experience.

- **Financial:** Encourage this person to think about a financial goal they have for the year, which could be to save for a family vacation or to invest in the stock market. Once a goal is set, have them consider podcasts, articles or online learning that will teach them methods to reach that goal.

- **Physical:** Incorporating deep learning into their workout program will make it easy for this person to maintain a regular routine. Coach them to save their favorite daily reading, podcasts or audiobook for their workout.

- **Community:** This person will thrive volunteering in a local library, museum or historical society. They will also be highly valued by community leadership when they take deep dives into current issues and report what they have discovered.

MAXIMIZER

People exceptionally talented in the Maximizer theme focus on strengths as a way to stimulate personal and group excellence. They seek to transform something strong into something superb.

- **Career:** Put this person on your best and most important assignments. They thrive when they take good projects and make them extraordinary.

- **Social:** Others are drawn to this person's natural ability to spot their potential. Maximizers get the most satisfaction from making the best even better.

- **Financial:** This person will seek to maximize their investments and will want to make a good financial plan better — and they will squeeze every ounce out of a stock portfolio.

- **Physical:** When this person enters a gym, they are going to look for ways to improve their routine as well as everyone else's. They will pursue the best exercise and fitness plans for their needs and will push good workout partners to be better.

- **Community:** Challenge this person to join a charity or nonprofit that is already going well and take it to the next level.

POSITIVITY

People exceptionally talented in the Positivity theme have contagious enthusiasm. They are upbeat and can get others excited about what they are going to do.

- **Career:** When difficult situations arise at work, look to this person to find an opportunity in the problem. They naturally inject positive energy and inspiration to keep their coworkers motivated.

- **Social:** This person enjoys cheering others on. They can make even small accomplishments seem great. People feel better about themselves in their company. Coach them to minimize their time with negative people because it drains the energy out of them.

- **Financial:** This person will see the positive outcomes of their financial portfolio — to a fault. They will benefit from a strong financial adviser who will keep them grounded.

- **Physical:** This person's positive contribution will be of infinite value to any workout group they join. They gain energy by energizing others.

- **Community:** People are attracted to this person's contagious excitement. They will make an extraordinary and positive contribution to any cause — especially one they love.

RELATOR

People exceptionally talented in the Relator theme enjoy close relationships with others. They find deep satisfaction in working hard with friends to achieve a goal.

- **Career:** One-on-one engagements and team meetings are how this person bonds with colleagues. They will thrive in a workplace where friendships and trusting relationships are part of the culture.

- **Social:** This person will struggle in large groups where they don't know anyone. However, they will thrive when they are looking forward to spending time with or involved in work assignments with their best friends.

- **Financial:** This person will require a deep, meaningful relationship with their financial adviser. The power of the relationship is more valuable to them than the expertise.

- **Physical:** What will be most motivating to this person is membership at a small, boutique exercise studio, where they can more easily build relationships. They will enjoy taking fitness classes with a close friend.

- **Community:** When coaching this person to get involved in the community, encourage them to bring a best friend along. There is no limit to their community involvement as long as it's connected through a small network of close friends.

RESPONSIBILITY

People exceptionally talented in the Responsibility theme take psychological ownership of what they say they will do. They are committed to stable values such as honesty and loyalty.

- **Career:** Colleagues can count on this person to meet their commitments. They always keep their word, and they thrive when they deliver on a big promise.

- **Social:** This person brings a sense of stability and integrity to relationships. Their commitment and follow-through on even the smallest promise attracts others to them because they are a rock of dependability.

- **Financial:** This person's sense of responsibility means they are naturally good at paying their bills on time and staying within budgets. Encourage them to use apps or other tools that make it easy for them to check their balances every day. They thrive when they keep all their financial commitments.

- **Physical:** An accountability partner will motivate this person because they will not want to let their partner down. Whether their goal is to lose weight or get more sleep, encourage them to share their goal with a friend so they can support each other and check in on their progress.

- **Community:** Light up this person's Responsibility theme by getting them to see that they can have an even bigger commitment. They will thrive when they understand their overarching responsibility to their community and country.

RESTORATIVE

People exceptionally talented in the Restorative theme are adept at dealing with problems. They are good at figuring out what is wrong and resolving it.

- **Career:** This person loves to find something that is broken and fix it. They like to look at a problem from all angles and find the root cause to solve it. They will thrive when you tell them, "The organization has a big problem that we need you to fix."

- **Social:** What attracts people to this person is that they can fix anything that is broken and will do it now — they draw energy from it. This is an appealing quality, and you should let them know it. Everyone needs a friend like them.

- **Financial:** There is no end to financial problems as markets, interest rates and individual needs change. This person thrives when asked how to fix financial problems, whether their own or others'.

- **Physical:** Encourage this person to think of their physical issues as problems they need to fix. They will be more successful when they think of improving their physical wellbeing this way.

- **Community:** Help this person identify the biggest problems in their community, and challenge them to get involved. The bigger and harder the problem, the more they will soar when analyzing it, pulling it apart, and finding the cause and solution.

SELF-ASSURANCE

People exceptionally talented in the Self-Assurance theme feel confident in their ability to take risks and manage their own lives. They have an inner compass that gives them certainty in their decisions.

- **Career:** Put this person in charge of starting a bold new initiative. They will thrive because they know they can do it.

- **Social:** This person can be intimidating. In social situations, coach them to ask other people their opinions as a way of building rapport.

- **Financial:** This person relies on gut instinct. However, their confidence in their own judgment can get them in financial trouble. Encourage them to slow down and seek the opinions of financial experts before making a big decision.

- **Physical:** It is likely that this person takes on ambitious challenges, whether running a marathon, signing up for a 50-mile bike race or attempting to lose weight. Help them benchmark their progress so that their Self-Assurance doesn't get too far ahead of their achievement.

- **Community:** This person can inspire others to act when all seems lost. Suggest that they get involved in a group they feel passionate about, where their natural self-confidence and drive can push people to find a path forward.

SIGNIFICANCE

People exceptionally talented in the Significance theme want to make a big impact. They are independent and prioritize projects based on how much influence they will have on their organization or people around them.

- **Career:** Consider this person to lead the team when you have a project with high visibility and importance. They will be motivated to do their best work when they know others are watching.

- **Social:** Recognition as affirmation and respect is key for this person. They need to know they are admired by their circle of friends and family. Coach them to find a balance between seeking public recognition and giving it to others.

- **Financial:** This person will want to have an image of financial stability. Inspire them to live within their means and to avoid acting like they are much richer than they are. Their Significance will be better served through a legacy of giving back.

- **Physical:** This person wants to be a healthy role model. Encourage them to report to their constituencies when they hit new health milestones.

- **Community:** This person will want others to know what they are contributing to the community. Challenge them to get involved in initiatives that are high-profile and where they play a public role.

STRATEGIC

People exceptionally talented in the Strategic theme create alternative ways to proceed. Faced with any given scenario, they can quickly spot the relevant patterns and issues.

- **Career:** This person can sort through information and map the best route. Put them on projects or assignments that demand a plan no one else can figure out.

- **Social:** Where others see obstacles, this person sees a path forward. Encourage them to generously offer strategic advice to friends and family. They can identify options and solutions in virtually any situation, even social situations.

- **Financial:** In the absence of a strategic plan for their financial future, this person is likely to experience significant stress and anxiety. Coach them to do their best strategic work on this key wellbeing element.

- **Physical:** Getting in 10,000 steps a day in a busy life is more achievable for this person when it is part of a larger plan for overall wellbeing. Ask them once a week, "How is your health strategy going?"

- **Community:** Communities, neighborhoods, nonprofits and charities — without exception — need better strategies. This person will thrive when asked to help with any strategic planning, and any community organization will greatly appreciate their talents.

WOO

People exceptionally talented in the Woo theme love the challenge of meeting new people and winning them over. They derive satisfaction from breaking the ice and making a connection with someone.

- **Career:** This person experiences a boost to their wellbeing when they meet people for the first time. They need to be in a job that requires regularly interacting with many new people.

- **Social:** This person may not need coaching in this element of wellbeing because they thrive so naturally in it. Encourage them to use this strength every day because it fuels *all* of their wellbeing.

- **Financial:** Advise this person to build fun relationships and have inspiring conversations with experts who can help them tackle sometimes difficult and dull financial subjects.

- **Physical:** This person will thrive when asked to recruit participants to the annual company "Olympics" day or 5K fun run. They love going door to door meeting and inviting people they do not know.

- **Community:** This person thrives when bringing people together who have never met. They are natural networkers. Coach them to use this rare gift to build constituencies for causes they love.

Appendix 2:
Manager Resource Guide to the Five Elements of Wellbeing

———

Wellbeing is the catalyst organizations need to cultivate engaged, thriving employees who perform at their best every day. Your employees' wellbeing influences every aspect of your business performance.

Use this guide to learn more about each of the five elements of wellbeing: career, social, financial, physical and community. The discussion topics will help you influence your own wellbeing and the wellbeing of others, including your team, by asking better questions and effectively listening to what your employees are saying.

Career Wellbeing: You Like What You Do Every Day

People with high career wellbeing wake up every morning with something to look forward to doing that day. Whether they are working at home or in an office, classroom or cubicle, they have the opportunity to use their strengths each day and to make progress. Those with thriving career wellbeing have a purpose to their life and a plan to reach their goals. In most cases, they have a leader or manager who makes them enthusiastic about the future and friends who share their passion.

Use these insights, conversation starters and discussion questions to create a workplace where everyone can thrive in this element of wellbeing.

Ask Yourself:

- What do I enjoy most about my job?

- What goals will I achieve today?

- Looking ahead to my day, what gives me the most energy?

- How will what I do today connect to my organization's overall mission or purpose?

- Which of my strengths will I use today?

- Would my team benefit from additional information about our purpose and goals?

- Is the vision for the future clear to my team? Where or how can I add clarity?

- Do I encourage my team members to pause and celebrate their achievements?

- How can I align each individual's developmental goals with team projects?

- How can I better position individuals to use their strengths every day?

Ask Your Team Members:

- Of all the things you do well in your job, which ones do you do best?

- If you could make one change for the better, what would it be?

- How does our work fulfill our purpose as a team?

- How will your work today fulfill your purpose?

- What parts of your role give you the most energy?

Take Action With These Best Practices:

- Identify the parts of your role that fulfill you the most, and look for opportunities to do them more often.

- Spend more time with the people you enjoy being around at work.

- Participate in activities that let you use your strengths every day.

- Identify purpose-filled moments and celebrate them.

- At the end of the day, pause and appreciate your accomplishments.

- Identify someone with a shared mission who encourages your growth, and spend more time with them.

Social Wellbeing: You Have Meaningful Friendships in Your Life

People with thriving social wellbeing have several close relationships that make their life more productive and enjoyable. They are surrounded by people who encourage their development and growth. They deliberately spend time — on average about six hours a day — investing in their relationships. They make time for gatherings and trips that strengthen those relationships even more. As a result, people with thriving social wellbeing have great relationships, which gives them positive energy on a daily basis.

Use these insights, conversation starters and discussion questions to create a workplace where everyone can thrive in this element of wellbeing.

Ask Yourself:

- How do I show the people who are most important to me that I care about them?

- How can I spend more time with a friend or colleague today?

- Who would enjoy hearing from me?

- How can I provide friendship and support to someone?

- How am I modeling social wellbeing to my team?

- What can I do to show others that I appreciate them today?

- How can I create more opportunities for my team to connect socially?

Ask Your Team Members:

- Do we spend enough social time together as a team?
- Who needs your support and attention today?
- How do we celebrate each other's personal and professional successes?
- How do we show our support for each other's social wellbeing?

Take Action With These Best Practices:

- Create opportunities for people to learn about one another — their work and lives.
- Get to know each other's personal hobbies and interests.
- Celebrate each other's personal and professional successes.
- Share individual goals so team members can provide support and encouragement.
- Schedule time for team social events or activities.
- Spend six hours a day socializing with friends, family and colleagues. This time includes phone, email and other communication whether you are at work or home.
- Mix social time with physical activity. For example, take a long walk with a friend so you can motivate each other to be healthy.

Financial Wellbeing: You Manage Your Money Well

People with high financial wellbeing manage their personal finances well and spend their money wisely. They buy experiences instead of just material possessions, and they give to others instead of always spending on themselves. At a basic level, they are satisfied with their overall standard of living. Their successful strategies result in financial security, which eliminates daily stress and worry caused by debt. This allows them to do what they want to do when they want to do it. They have the financial freedom to spend more time with the people they like to be around.

Use these insights, conversation starters and discussion questions to create a workplace where everyone can thrive in this element of wellbeing.

Ask Yourself:

- What are my financial goals?

- What additional tools, skills or resources do I need to achieve my financial goals?

- How might a new approach to my finances help me improve my wellbeing?

- What can I do today that will have a positive influence on my long-term financial goals?

- How do I convey a sense of fairness and equity when discussing compensation with employees?

- How can I promote opportunities to improve my team's financial wellbeing?

- How can I initiate peer group discussions so my team can learn financial strategies from each other?

- Does my team know what organizational financial resources are available to them?

Ask Your Team Members:

- Do we encourage each other to have enjoyable experiences such as a great vacation?

- What financial educational opportunities are available to us?

- How can we support each other in our pursuit of our financial goals?

- What financial habits could we modify to enhance our individual financial wellbeing?

- What is the best way for us to learn financial wellbeing strategies from one another?

Take Action With These Best Practices:

- Brainstorm new habits that are cost-effective and promote saving money.

- Encourage each other to bring lunch from home rather than eating out.

- Celebrate team members' financial achievements.

- Buy experiences — such as vacations and outings with friends or family — because experiences last, while material purchases fade.

- Spend your money on others instead of only on yourself.

- Establish default systems (automated payments and savings) that will reduce your daily worries about money.

Physical Wellbeing: You Have Energy to Get Things Done

People with thriving physical wellbeing manage their health well. They exercise regularly, and as a result, they feel better. They make good dietary choices, which keeps their energy high throughout the day and sharpens their thinking. They get enough sleep to process what they learned the day before and to get a good start on the next day. People with thriving physical wellbeing feel better and live longer.

Use these insights, conversation starters and discussion questions to create a workplace where everyone can thrive in this element of wellbeing.

Ask Yourself:

- What can I do today to boost my energy?

- Think about days when I have had the most physical and mental energy. What do they have in common?

- What new habits could I start to support my physical wellbeing goals?

- How do I incorporate activity into my workday?

- Where do I need help making progress in my physical wellbeing efforts?

- What can I do today to support my team members' physical wellbeing?

- How can I help my team incorporate more physical activity into the workday?

Ask Your Team Members:

- How do our work areas and schedules support our physical wellbeing goals?

- How can we support each other's physical wellbeing?

- Where can we add physical wellbeing elements to our day?

- What physical wellbeing obstacles do we encounter at work?

Take Action With These Best Practices:

- Add physical wellbeing activities to your team meetings or monthly calendar.

- Hold "walk and talk" meetings when possible, rather than sitting.

- Build in short physical wellbeing breaks throughout the day to avoid long periods of sedentary time.

- Ask a teammate to be a physical wellbeing accountability buddy.

- Participate in physical wellbeing events in the community together.

- Get at least 20 minutes of physical activity each day — ideally in the morning to improve your mood throughout the day.

- Sleep enough to feel well-rested (generally seven to eight hours) but not too long (more than nine hours).

- Set positive defaults when you shop for groceries. Load up on natural instead of processed foods.

Community Wellbeing: You Like Where You Live

People with high community wellbeing feel safe and secure where they live. They take pride in their community and feel that it's headed in the right direction. This often results in their wanting to give back and make a lasting contribution to society. These people have identified the areas where they can volunteer based on their strengths and passions, and they tell others about these interests to connect with the right groups and causes. Their contributions to the community may start small, but over time, lead to more involvement and have a profound impact. These efforts create communities we cannot imagine living without.

Use these insights, conversation starters and discussion questions to create a workplace where everyone can thrive in this element of wellbeing.

Ask Yourself:

- What makes me proud about where I live?

- How can my community get better? What can I help change?

- What is one community event or activity that I would enjoy getting involved in?

- How can I apply my passions and interests to organizations in my community?

- How can I recognize my organization's or team's community involvement?

- How can I be more supportive of my team members' involvement in community events?

Ask Your Team Members:

- What do you feel passionate about in your communities?

- How can we get involved in our communities?

- What shared community interests do we have?

- What are some things we can do as a team to show our support for our communities?

- How can we be ambassadors for our organization's community wellbeing opportunities?

- How does the work we do every day have an impact on our communities?

Take Action With These Best Practices:

- Volunteer for a community event you feel passionate about as a team.

- Serve as volunteers or board members for organizations that are important to your team.

- Establish partnerships with community organizations that share your team's purpose.

- Identify how you can contribute to your community based on your personal mission.

- Tell people about your passions and interests so they can connect you with relevant groups and causes.

- Join a community group or event. Even if you start small, start now.

Appendix 3:

Technical Report: The Research and Development of Gallup's Five Elements of Wellbeing

---

Purpose

Gallup's goal in developing the five elements of wellbeing was to use current science to create a comprehensive, reliable, valid, concise and actionable set of constructs that managers and individuals could use to provide insights and track their wellbeing over time. Our team of scientists sought to identify wellbeing dimensions that explain differences in wellbeing for people in diverse life situations and that represent areas in which individuals can take action to improve their wellbeing. Wellbeing is *all the things that are important to how we think about and experience our lives.*

History of Instrument Design

Development of the five elements of wellbeing occurred in three iterations or phases:

- Phase 1: Review of Historical Gallup Wellbeing Research
- Phase 2: Gallup Global Research and Analysis
- Phase 3: Pilot Research for the Wellbeing Constructs
  - Pilot 1: Item testing across diverse groups
  - Pilot 2: Refinement of measures/constructs in international samples
- Phase 4: Meta-Analysis of the Five Elements of Wellbeing Across Countries
- Phase 5: Additional Confirmatory Analyses

Phase 1: Review of Historical Gallup Wellbeing Research

The foundation for the questions in Gallup's five wellbeing element measures is based in the work of George Gallup and his colleagues, which began in the 1930s. In 1960, Dr. Gallup published a study and subsequent book titled *The Secrets of Long Life*. Gallup research into wellbeing and human needs and satisfaction continued through the 1960s, 1970s and 1980s.

In the 1990s, Gallup initiated a series of landmark studies. One nationwide study began in China in 1994, long before any other public opinion work was initiated in that country. In 1996, Gallup began a similar nationwide study in India and conducted baseline studies in Israel and the Palestinian Territories in 1999. Also in the 1990s, Gallup conducted several studies of community vitality and satisfaction with life. Between 2001 and 2007, Gallup conducted tens of thousands of interviews with residents of nations that are predominantly Muslim or have substantial Muslim populations. The first truly global research study (representing more than 98% of the world's adult population in more than 150 countries) began in 2005 and continues today.

Many of the question items from past Gallup research are used in or influenced question wording in the wellbeing measurement. These included questions that measure basic needs such as safety, food and shelter, and higher-level needs such as quality of work, health, relationships, economics and community involvement. Questions were reviewed for evidence of reliability, validity and applicability to individual intervention (rather than policy-oriented issues).

Phase 2: Gallup Global Research and Analysis

Prior to development of the Gallup global study, thousands of possible questions were considered. The initial pilot survey included 130 items that took respondents 30-35 minutes to complete. This survey was later refined based on statistical analysis to include 100 items that took respondents 20-25 minutes to complete. The seven core indexes assessed are Law and Order, Food and Shelter, Work, Personal Economy, Personal Health, Citizen Engagement, and Wellbeing. The global study now includes substantially more indexes, each of which have been tested for reliability and validity evidence.

Sampling and Data Collection Methodology

With few exceptions, all samples are probability based and nationally representative of the resident population aged 15 and older. The coverage area is the entire country including rural areas, and the sampling frame represents the entire civilian, noninstitutionalized, aged 15 and older population of the entire country. Exceptions include areas where the safety of interviewing staff is threatened; scarcely populated islands in some countries; and areas that interviewers can reach only by foot, animal or small boat.

Telephone surveys are used in countries where telephone coverage represents at least 80% of the population or is the customary survey methodology. In Central and Eastern Europe, as well as in the developing world, including much of Latin America, the former Soviet Union countries, nearly all of Asia, the Middle East and Africa, an area frame design is used for face-to-face interviewing.

The typical global survey in a country consists of at least 1,000 surveys of individuals. In some large countries, oversamples are collected in major cities or areas of special interest. Although infrequent, there are some instances in which the sample size is between 500 and 1,000.

In addition to the immense coverage of the global study (now more than 98% of the world's population), the concept of wellbeing is considered from a diverse perspective.

Historically, definitions of wellbeing have fallen into two broad categories. The first category consists of traditional neoclassic measures such as income, GDP, life expectancy and poverty rates. The second includes the subjective or psychological measures of wellbeing that seek to measure how people feel about their lives. Based on more recent research, the second category can be separated into two general types: those measures that tap into the evaluating or remembering self and those that tap into the experiencing self.

Different Measures of Wellbeing

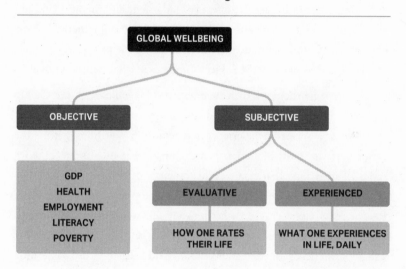

Nobel laureate Daniel Kahneman and University of Illinois at Urbana-Champaign psychology professor Ed Diener have been influential in conceiving the contemporary views of wellbeing. In the journal article "Guidelines for National Indicators of Subjective Well-Being and Ill-Being," Diener defines subjective wellbeing as "all of the various types of evaluations, both positive and negative, that people make of their lives. It includes reflective cognitive evaluations, such as life satisfaction and work satisfaction, interest and engagement, and affective reactions to life events, such as joy and sadness." Similarly, in the book *The Science of Well-Being: Integrating Neurobiology, Psychology,*

and Social Science, Kahneman makes note of the distinction between "experienced well-being" and "evaluative well-being." Experienced wellbeing is concerned with momentary affective states and the way people feel about experiences in real time, while evaluative wellbeing is the way they remember their experiences after they are over. Experienced wellbeing seeks to bypass the effects of judgment and memory and has historically been measured using the experience sampling method or the day reconstruction method — both of which seek to capture feelings and emotions as close to the subject's immediate experience as possible.

Inspired by the work of Kahneman and his colleagues, the Gallup global study adapted these methods to a large-scale survey environment by framing a series of experience and emotion questions within the context of the past 24 hours. For example, respondents are asked a series of questions that relate to experiences of positive and negative emotions, including feelings of enjoyment, happiness, stress and anger. Respondents are also asked whether they felt well-rested the previous day, whether they were treated with respect, smiled or laughed a lot, had a lot of energy, worried about money, and learned or did something interesting. They are also asked about their time use, such as the amount of time spent socially or commuting to work.

Numerous reports and findings from the Gallup global study can be accessed on Gallup.com.

Using our definition of wellbeing as *all the things that are important to how we think about and experience our lives*, we then studied how various elements of wellbeing explained measures of life evaluation/judgment and daily experience.

Phase 3: Pilot Research for the Wellbeing Constructs

Phase 3 began with a review of individual-level data from Gallup's global study. We assessed the generalizability of important key wellbeing domains through regression analysis. Additionally, we reviewed wellbeing literature and conducted qualitative interviews to hypothesize individually and organizationally actionable areas. Items were written and initially tested between 2004 and 2007. Follow-up pilot testing of the web-based field assessment was conducted between 2007 and 2009.

From this exploratory research, 340 wellbeing items were generated for testing, covering many different life domains and experiences, including: career; interests; passions; life balance; enjoyment of work; satisfaction with boss; stress; purpose; mentors; strengths; family; friends; social time; marriage; children; religion; faith; spirituality; equality; goals; basic needs; housing; income; physical security; financial security; spending habits; peer group; fatigue; diet; exercise; energy; sleep habits; pain; body image; illnesses; sick days; safety; access to food, water and clean air; community engagement; and contributions to society, in addition to other areas.

Based on exploratory factor analysis, five broad wellbeing dimensions were hypothesized. These dimensions capture the majority of the variance in wellbeing outcome variables such as overall life evaluation in the present, hope for the future and daily experiences:

- **Career or occupational wellbeing:** You like what you do every day.

- **Social wellbeing:** You have meaningful friendships in your life.

- **Financial wellbeing:** You manage your money well.

- **Physical wellbeing:** You have energy to get things done.

- **Community wellbeing:** You like where you live.

As the following chart shows, the 340 items were dispersed across five subsamples and tested for reliability and validity evidence.

Pilot 1: Sample Size by Sample/Subgroups

U.S. Residents – Panel (N = 10,544)

CAREER	(n = 2,389)
Not employed	388
Full-time student	300
Homemaker	386
Part-time/not full-time student	419
Retired	473
Employed full time	423

PHYSICAL	(n = 2,677)
HEALTHY	1,344
<50	462
50-64	500
65+	382
UNHEALTHY	1,333
<50	389
50-64	462
65+	482

COMMUNITY/SAFETY	(n = 1,254)
Rural	427
Urban	403
Suburban	424

FINANCIAL	(n = 2,080)
<$25,000	369
$25,000 - $49,999	401
$50,000 - $99,999	411
$100,000 - $199,999	429
$200,000+	470

RELATIONSHIP	(n = 2,144)
Married	436
Widowed	438
Separated/divorced	439
Single/never married	420
Living with a partner	411

We oversampled particular subgroups of the Gallup Panel to maximize information on a diverse set of individuals within each wellbeing dimension (people in various career and financial situations; living in assorted locales; and with differing age, health and relationship status). This allowed us to learn which facets of wellbeing were most important in a variety of contexts. Within each wellbeing dimension, we studied which questions best differentiated those with high versus low wellbeing.

Four primary dependent variables were considered:

1. Life evaluation: present (0-10 scale)

2. Life evaluation: future (0-10 scale)

3. Daily experiences: enjoyment, happiness, physical pain, worry, sadness, stress, boredom, anger, contentment

4. Exceeding wildest expectations: "Up to this point, my life has exceeded my wildest expectations" (1-5 agreement scale)

There were five separate surveys designed for this phase of research (one for each wellbeing dimension). Analysis was conducted within each subsample within each dimension. The goal was to maximize information for each wellbeing dimension by selecting the best items for the next phase of research, considering validity and reliability evidence.

For example, the Cronbach's alpha reliability exceeded 0.70 (range of 0.72 to 0.91) for each dimension based on retained items, and reliability was consistently high across the subsamples within each dimension. The following table shows the correlations to the four criterion variables for each dimension (the validities did not vary substantially across subsamples).

Pilot 1: Validity Estimates

Wellbeing Dimension	Life Evaluation	Future	Daily Experiences	Wildest Expectations
Career	0.56	0.47	0.53	0.60
Social	0.54	0.45	0.49	0.55
Financial	0.65	0.48	0.48	0.53
Physical	0.46	0.33	0.46	0.34
Community	0.49	0.37	0.44	0.47

A total of 164 items were retained for the next phase of research, which included a random sample of 2,135 adults aged 18 and older and 172 youths aged 13-17. For this phase of the research, we combined items across wellbeing dimensions to assess the independence of the factors.

The list of items was further refined based on confirmatory factor analysis and further criterion-related validity study, which resulted in 120 items spread across the five wellbeing dimensions. The instrument was then translated into seven languages for further international testing (Chinese-Traditional, Chinese-Simplified, French-European, German, Japanese, Spanish-Latin American and English-Great Britain).

Factor analysis indicated five distinct factors, each with eigenvalues above 2.0 and each with reliabilities above 0.75 for adults and youths. The average intercorrelation between dimensions was 0.51 for adults and 0.56 for youths. Validity estimates were of similar magnitude to those found in the earlier pilot studies and were generalizable for adults aged 18 and older and youths aged 13-17.

The field instrument contained 10 items per wellbeing dimension, for a total of 50 scored items plus additional research items.

Pilot 2: Reliability and Validity Estimates

DIMENSION	RELIABILITY	VALIDITY				
		Life Evaluation	Future	Daily Experiences	Wildest Expectations	Sick Days
Career	0.85	0.58	0.46	0.48	0.60	-0.21
Social	0.86	0.52	0.38	0.45	0.50	-0.12
Financial	0.84	0.63	0.38	0.38	0.51	-0.19
Physical	0.83	0.50	0.37	0.46	0.43	-0.41
Community	0.77	0.38	0.25	0.36	0.40	-0.11

Partial Correlations* With Outcome Variables

Wellbeing Dimension	Life Evaluation	Future	Daily Experiences	Wildest Expectations	Sick Days
Career	**0.22**	**0.18**	**0.15**	**0.31**	0.00
Social	**0.09**	0.04	**0.09**	**0.06**	**0.09**
Financial	**0.40**	**0.19**	**0.13**	**0.19**	**0.05**
Physical	**0.13**	**0.08**	**0.24**	0.02	**0.36**
Community	0.00	**0.05**	**0.11**	**0.08**	0.02

* Partial correlations controlling for gender, age, income, education, marital status, employment status, race and the other four wellbeing dimensions. Partial correlations in bold have 95% confidence intervals that do not overlap with zero.

Regression analyses were also conducted by first entering demographic variables into the equation (age, gender, employment status, marital status, race, education level and income level) and then entering each of the wellbeing dimensions. Dependent variables, as previously studied, included life evaluation: present and future, daily experiences, and exceeding wildest expectations. For adults and youths, each dimension accounted for unique information, beyond demographics and other wellbeing dimensions, in multiple dependent variables. For instance, all five dimensions accounted for unique variance in daily experiences. The first four dimensions (career, social, financial and physical) each accounted for unique variance in life evaluation: future. The first three dimensions (career, social and financial) and community each accounted for unique variance in exceeding wildest expectations. Of the five dimensions, the two most highly correlated are career and social wellbeing, correlating 0.69 for adults and 0.75 for youths. As such, they may be the most interchangeable in their impact on wellbeing outcomes.

The following table shows the Multiple Rs for demographics and the total model (demographics plus wellbeing dimensions).

Regression: Multiple R

The following are Multiple Rs for demographics and the total model (demographics plus wellbeing dimensions)

	Life Evaluation	Future	Daily Experiences	Wildest Expectations	Sick Days
Demographics	0.25	0.24	0.17	0.29	0.22
+ Wellbeing dimensions	0.72	0.54	0.62	0.66	0.46

It is clear that the five wellbeing dimensions, while not explaining all of what makes up a great life for all individuals, describe a great deal across multiple wellbeing outcome variables. They also add substantially to other situational or demographic variables in explaining wellbeing.

After translation into seven languages (Chinese-Traditional [n = 829], Chinese-Simplified [n = 3,186], French-European [n = 288], German [n = 522], Japanese [n = 3,085], Spanish-Latin American [n = 1,210] and English-Great Britain [n = 731]), we conducted confirmatory factor analysis and reliability, validity and generalizability analyses. Based on confirmatory factor analysis, the average item-factor loading ranged from 0.52 to 0.58 across the languages. We correlated the item-factor loadings across languages, and the strength of the individual item-factor loadings was very similar across languages (mean r of 50 item-factor loadings across languages = 0.79). SRMR (standardized root mean squared residual) fit ranged from 0.06 to 0.071 across languages, indicating acceptable fit of the factor model to the data. The mean item-dimension corrected correlation (corrected for part-whole overlap) was 50% higher than the mean item correlation to other dimensions. Additionally, the pattern of intercorrelations among dimensions (that is, how dimensions related to each other) was similar across languages. (The correlation matrices agreed across languages; mean r = 0.89.) The reliability of the dimensions was also similar across languages.

Mean Reliability Across Languages

WELLBEING DIMENSION	MEAN RELIABILITY
Career	0.86
Social	0.85
Financial	0.75
Physical	0.77
Community	0.72
Overall	0.93

We also conducted meta-analysis to understand the generalizability of each wellbeing dimension's relationship to each of the criterion variables across languages. The correlation of each dimension to life evaluation: future, daily experiences, exceeding wildest expectations and sick days was in the hypothesized direction and generalizable across languages. This provides strong evidence of the generalizability of the five core constructs across various languages.

Phase 4: Meta-Analysis of the Five Wellbeing Elements Across Countries

As part of the ongoing validation of the five wellbeing elements discovered during phases 1-3, key items from each of the five elements were included in Gallup's World Poll, fielded from February 2009 to March 2010. This gave us the opportunity to:

1. estimate the relationship between each of the five wellbeing elements (career, social, financial, physical and community) and six dependent variables (present life evaluation, future life evaluation, daily wellbeing, number of unhealthy days in the past 30 days, general health problems and giving) across world regions.

2. examine the moderation effect of country-level GDP and location/region on the relationship between each of the wellbeing elements and the dependent variables.

3. estimate the practical meaning of the relationships.

Methods

The dataset included nationally representative samples of the population aged 15 and older in 117 countries from the Gallup World Poll, representing more than 95% of the world's adult population. A total of 120,239 interviews were conducted from February 2009 through March 2010, using face-to-face or telephone methodology. The Gallup World Poll includes a core set of 100 wellbeing items. In 2009, based on research that found five important subjective factors (elements) of individual wellbeing (Rath & Harter, 2010), five items were added to the World Poll (one item that best explained variance in each of the five elements: career, social, financial, physical and community wellbeing). We statistically calculated the individual-level relationship between the five wellbeing items and outcome variables. Six outcomes were studied: present life evaluation, future life evaluation, daily wellbeing, number of unhealthy days in the past 30 days, general health problems and giving. Moderation was examined across country-level GDP and location/region categorization.

Results

Each of the five wellbeing elements explained meaningful variance in each of the six outcomes studied. Results indicated high generalizability — meaning the correlations were largely consistent across different countries after controlling for demographic differences.

Meta-Analytic True Score Partial Correlations After Controlling for Demographics

OUTCOME VARIABLES	INDEPENDENT VARIABLES				
	CAREER	SOCIAL	FINANCIAL	PHYSICAL	COMMUNITY
Present Life Evaluation	0.34	0.27	0.39	0.25	0.17
Future Life Evaluation	0.17	0.35	0.33	0.27	0.21
Daily Wellbeing	0.43	0.37	0.30	0.39	0.23
Number of Unhealthy Days	-0.21	-0.12	-0.14	-0.52	-0.07
General Health Problems (Yes)	-0.15	-0.11	-0.10	-0.52	-0.06
Giving (Yes)	0.10	0.11	0.07	0.06	0.04

Key findings: This table summarizes the true score partial correlations for each wellbeing element-outcome variable combination. While the magnitude of the correlations varies, after controlling for demographic variables, all of the true score correlations are in the hypothesized direction.

Respondents with higher wellbeing in all five elements reported higher life evaluations (future and present), better daily experiences, fewer sick days and health problems, and higher likelihood of giving. Those with high career wellbeing reported fewer than half as many unhealthy days and were 39% less likely to report chronic health problems compared with those with low career wellbeing. Those with high social wellbeing were 17% more likely to report giving compared with those with low social wellbeing. Those with high financial wellbeing reported higher life satisfaction compared with those with low financial wellbeing.

The relationship between the five wellbeing elements and wellbeing outcome variables at the individual level is substantial and generalizable across countries. This provides further evidence of the universality of the five core wellbeing elements. More detailed analyses are available in a separate Gallup technical report (Agrawal & Harter, 2011).

Phase 5: Additional Confirmatory Analyses

Using a longitudinal sample of approximately 11,500 U.S. Gallup Panel members (5,500 who were employed), Gallup explored the causal relationships among the five wellbeing elements and life evaluations, daily experiences, employee engagement, workplace turnover and health outcomes (Harter & Agrawal, 2012). We evaluated causality using a series of longitudinal regression analyses (linear and logistic). Findings indicated that while causality was reciprocal, the five wellbeing elements were predictive of life evaluations, daily experiences, employee engagement, turnover intentions, actual turnover, unhealthy days and new incidence of disease burden (e.g., anxiety/depression, hypertension, sleep disorders, diabetes and obesity).

Further research explored the validity and reliability of measures of the five elements across 13,000 individuals in three independent samples (Sears, Agrawal, Sidney, Castle, Rula, Coberley, Witters, Pope, & Harter, 2014). The research further established significant relationships with health and performance outcomes. The study further substantiated the factor analytic model and the construct and convergent validity properties of the five wellbeing elements using multiple sets of items. The study found substantial relationships between the five elements and job performance, absenteeism and hospital admissions outcomes.

Summary

The five elements of wellbeing were developed based on a foundation of world research and a long Gallup history of studying wellbeing. These five wellbeing elements are our best attempt to summarize what makes most people's lives and days fulfilling. Gallup designed them to create awareness of measurable and actionable areas of an individual's life. While a great deal has gone into the science of wellbeing to date, future research will provide substantial insight into how it is most effectively applied and how measurement can be continually refined to provide the best insights, with the goal to improve the wellbeing of the world's citizens.

References

Agrawal, S. & Harter, J. K. (2011). *Wellbeing meta-analysis: A worldwide study of the relationship between the five elements of wellbeing and life evaluation, daily experiences, health, and giving.* Gallup Technical Report.

Cantril, H. (1965). *The pattern of human concerns.* New Brunswick, NJ: Rutgers University Press.

Diener, E. (2005). Guidelines for national indicators of subjective well-being and ill-being. *Journal of Happiness Studies, 7,* 397-404.

The Gallup Organization. (2007). *The state of global well-being.* New York: Author.

Gallup, G., & Hill, E. (1960). *The secrets of long life.* New York: Bernard Geis.

Harter, J. K., & Agrawal, S. (2012). Causal relationships among wellbeing elements and life, work, and health outcomes. Gallup Technical Report.

Kahneman, D., Diener, E., & Schwarz, N. (Eds.). (1998). *Wellbeing: The foundations of hedonic psychology.* New York: Russell Sage Foundation.

Kahneman, D., & Riis, J. (2005). Living and thinking about it: Two perspectives on life. In F. Huppert, N. Baylis, & B. Kaverne (Eds.), *The science of well-being: Integrating neurobiology, psychology, and social science* (pp. 285-304). Oxford, United Kingdom: Oxford University Press.

Rath, T., & Harter, J. (2010). *Wellbeing: The five essential elements.* Gallup Press.

Sears, L. E., Agrawal, S., Sidney, J. A., Castle, P. H., Rula, E. Y., Coberley, C. R., Witters, D., Pope, J. E., & Harter, J. K. (2014). The well-being 5: Development and validation of a diagnostic instrument to improve population well-being. *Population Health Management, 17*(6), 357-365.

Appendix 4:

The Relationship Between Engagement at Work and Organizational Outcomes

---

2020 Q12® Meta-Analysis: 10th Edition

James K. Harter, Ph.D., Gallup

Frank L. Schmidt, Ph.D., University of Iowa

Sangeeta Agrawal, M.S., Gallup

Anthony Blue, M.A., Gallup

Stephanie K. Plowman, M.A., Gallup

Patrick Josh, M.A., Gallup

Jim Asplund, M.A., Gallup

OCTOBER 2020

Acknowledgements

The authors thank Marie-Lou Almeida, Jeevika Galhotra, Rujuta Gandhi, Julie Griffiths, Ryan Gottfredson, Domonique Hodge, Diana Lu, Shane McFeely, Marco Nink, John Reimnitz, Chayanun Saransomrurtai, Puneet Singh and Ben Wigert for contributing important new research studies to this ongoing meta-analysis.

Copyright Standards

Table of Contents

Executive Summary

Objective

Business and work units in the same organization vary substantially in their levels of engagement and performance. The purpose of this study was to examine the:

1. true relationship between employee engagement and performance in 276 organizations

2. consistency or generalizability of the relationship between employee engagement and performance across organizations

3. practical meaning of the findings for executives and managers

Methods

We accumulated 456 research studies across 276 organizations in 54 industries, with employees in 96 countries. Within each study, we statistically calculated the business-/work-unit-level relationship between employee engagement and performance outcomes that the organizations supplied. In total, we were able to study 112,312 business and work units that included 2,708,538 employees. We studied 11 outcomes: customer loyalty/engagement, profitability, productivity, turnover, safety incidents, absenteeism, shrinkage, patient safety incidents, quality (defects), wellbeing and organizational citizenship.

Individual studies often contain small sample sizes and idiosyncrasies that distort the interpretation of results. Meta-analysis is a statistical technique that is useful in combining results of studies with seemingly disparate findings, correcting for sampling, measurement error and other study artifacts to understand the true relationship with greater precision.

We applied Hunter-Schmidt meta-analysis methods to 456 research studies to estimate the true relationship between engagement and each performance measure and to test for generalizability. After conducting meta-analysis, we examined the practical meaning of the relationships by conducting utility analysis.

Results

Employee engagement is related to each of the 11 performance outcomes studied. Results indicate high generalizability, which means the correlations were consistent across different organizations. The true score correlation between employee engagement and composite performance is 0.49. Across companies, business/work units scoring in the top half on employee engagement more than double their odds of success compared with those in the bottom half. Those at the 99th percentile have nearly five times the success rate of those at the first percentile.

Median percent differences between top-quartile and bottom-quartile units were:

- 10% in customer loyalty/engagement

- 23% in profitability

- 18% in productivity (sales)

- 14% in productivity (production records and evaluations)

- 18% in turnover for high-turnover organizations (those with more than 40% annualized turnover)

- 43% in turnover for low-turnover organizations (those with 40% or lower annualized turnover)

- 64% in safety incidents (accidents)

- 81% in absenteeism

- 28% in shrinkage (theft)

- 58% in patient safety incidents (mortality and falls)

- 41% in quality (defects)

- 66% in wellbeing (net thriving employees)

- 13% in organizational citizenship (participation)

Conclusion

The relationship between engagement and performance at the business/work unit level is substantial and highly generalizable across organizations. Employee engagement is related to each of 11 performance outcomes. This means that practitioners can apply the Q^{12} measure in a variety of situations with confidence that the measure captures important performance-related information.

Introduction

Foreword

In the 1930s, George Gallup began a worldwide study of human needs and satisfactions. He pioneered the development of scientific sampling processes to measure public opinion. In addition to his polling work, Dr. Gallup completed landmark research on wellbeing, studying the factors common among people who lived to be 95 and older (Gallup & Hill, 1959). Over the next several decades, Dr. Gallup and his colleagues conducted numerous polls throughout the world, covering many aspects of people's lives. His early world polls dealt with topics such as family, religion, politics, personal happiness, economics, health, education, safety and attitudes toward work. In the 1970s, Dr. Gallup reported that less than half of those employed in North America were highly satisfied with their work (Gallup, 1976). Work satisfaction was even lower in Western Europe, Latin America, Africa and the Far East.

Satisfaction at work has become a widespread focus for researchers. In addition to Dr. Gallup's early work, the topic of job satisfaction has been studied and written about in more than 10,000 articles and publications. Because most people spend a high percentage of their waking hours at work, studies of the workplace are of great interest to psychologists, sociologists, economists, anthropologists and physiologists. The process of managing and improving the workplace is crucial and presents great challenges to nearly every organization. So, it is vital that the instruments used to create change do, in fact, measure workplace dynamics that predict key outcomes — outcomes that a variety of organizational leaders would consider important. After all, organizational leaders are in the best position to create interest in and momentum for job satisfaction research.

Parallel to Dr. Gallup's early polling work, Don Clifton, a psychologist and professor at the University of Nebraska, began studying the causes of success in education and business. Dr. Clifton founded Selection Research, Inc. (SRI) in 1969. While most psychologists were busy studying dysfunction and the cause of disease, Dr. Clifton and his colleagues focused their careers on the science of strengths-based psychology, the study of what makes people flourish.

Their early discoveries led to hundreds of research studies focused on successful individuals and teams across a broad spectrum of industries and job types. In particular, research on successful learning and workplace environments led to numerous studies of successful teachers and managers. This work included extensive research on individual differences and the environments that best facilitate success. Early in their studies, the researchers discovered that simply measuring employees' satisfaction was insufficient to create sustainable change. Satisfaction needed to be specified in terms of its most important elements, and it needed to be measured and reported in a way that could be used by the people who could take action and create change.

Further research revealed that change happens most efficiently at a local level — at the level of the front-line, manager-led team. For executives, front-line teams are their direct reports, and for plant managers, front-line teams are the people they manage each day. Studying great managers, Gallup scientists learned that optimal decision-making happens when information regarding decisions is collected at a local level, close to the everyday action.

Dr. Clifton's work merged with Dr. Gallup's work in 1988, when Gallup and SRI combined, enabling the blending of progressive management science with top survey and polling science. Dr. Gallup and Dr. Clifton spent much of their lives studying people's opinions, attitudes, talents and behaviors. To do this, they wrote questions, recorded the responses, and studied which questions elicited differential responses and related to meaningful outcomes. In the case of survey research, some questions are unbiased and elicit meaningful opinions, while others do not. In the case of management research, some questions elicit responses that predict future performance, while others do not.

Developing the right questions is an iterative process in which scientists write questions and conduct analysis. The research and questions are refined and rephrased. Additional analysis is conducted. The questions are refined and rephrased again. And the process is repeated. Gallup has followed the iterative process in devising the survey tool that is the subject of this report, Gallup's Q^{12} instrument, which is designed to measure employee engagement conditions.

The next section provides an overview of the many decades of research that have gone into the development and validation of Gallup's Q^{12} employee engagement instrument. Following this overview, we present a meta-analysis of 456 research studies, exploring the relationship between employee engagement and performance across 276 organizations and 112,312 business/work units that include 2,708,538 employees.

Development of the Q^{12}

Beginning in the 1950s, Dr. Clifton started studying work and learning environments to determine the factors that contribute positively to those environments and that enable people to capitalize on their unique talents. It was through this early work that Dr. Clifton began using science and the study of strengths to research individuals' frames of reference and attitudes.

From the 1950s to the 1970s, Dr. Clifton continued his research of students, counselors, managers, teachers and employees. He used various rating scales and interview techniques to study individual differences, analyzing questions and factors that explain dissimilarities in people. The concepts he studied included "focusing on strengths versus weaknesses," "relationships," "personnel support," "friendships" and "learning." Various questions were written and tested, including many early versions of the Q^{12} items. Ongoing feedback techniques were first developed with the intent of asking questions, collecting data and encouraging ongoing discussion of the results to provide feedback and potential improvement — a measurement-based feedback process. To learn causes of employee turnover, exit interviews were conducted with employees who left organizations. A common reason for leaving an organization focused on the quality of the manager.

In the 1980s, Gallup scientists continued the iterative process by studying high-performing individuals and teams. Studies involved assessments of individual talents and workplace attitudes. As a starting point for questionnaire design, numerous qualitative analyses were conducted, including interviews and focus groups. Gallup researchers asked top-performing individuals or teams to describe their work environments and their thoughts, feelings and behaviors related to success.

The researchers used qualitative data to generate hypotheses and insights into the distinguishing factors leading to success. From these hypotheses, they wrote and tested questions. They also conducted numerous quantitative studies throughout the 1980s, including exit interviews, to continue to learn causes of employee turnover. Qualitative analyses such as focus groups and interviews formed the basis for lengthy and comprehensive employee surveys, called "Organizational Development Audits" or "Managing Attitudes for Excellence" surveys.

Many of these surveys included 100 to 200 items. Quantitative analyses included factor analyses to assess the dimensionality of the survey data; regression analyses to identify uniqueness and redundancies in the data; and criterion-related validity analyses to identify questions that correlate with meaningful outcomes such as overall satisfaction, commitment and productivity. The scientists developed feedback protocols to facilitate the feedback of survey results to managers and employees. Such protocols and their use in practice helped researchers learn which items were most useful in creating dialogue and stimulating change.

One outgrowth of a management research practice that was focused on talent and environment was the theory of talent maximization in an organization:

Per–Person Productivity = Talent x (Relationship + Right Expectation + Recognition/Reward)

These concepts would later become embedded in the foundational elements of the Q^{12}.

Over time, SRI and Gallup researchers conducted numerous studies of manager success patterns that focused on the talents of the manager and the environments that best facilitated success. By integrating knowledge of managerial talent with survey data on employee attitudes, scientists had a unique perspective on what it takes to build a successful workplace environment. Themes such as "individualized perception," "performance orientation," "mission," "recognition," "learning and growing," "expectations," and "the right fit" continued to emerge. In addition to studies of management, researchers conducted numerous studies with successful teachers, students and learning environments.

In the 1990s, the iterative process continued. During this time, Gallup researchers developed the first version of the Q^{12} ("The Gallup

Workplace Audit" or GWA) in an effort to efficiently capture the most important workplace attitudes. Qualitative and quantitative analyses continued. In that decade, more than 1,000 focus groups were conducted and hundreds of instruments were developed, many of them with several additional items. Scientists also continued to use exit interviews; these revealed the importance of the manager in retaining employees. Studies of the Q^{12} and other survey items were conducted in various countries throughout the world, including the United States, Canada, Mexico, Great Britain, Japan and Germany. Gallup researchers obtained international cross-cultural feedback on Gallup's core items, which provided context on the applicability of the items across different cultures. Various scale types were also tested, including variations of 5-point and dichotomous response options.

Quantitative analyses of survey data included descriptive statistics, factor analyses, discriminant analyses, criterion-related validity analyses, reliability analyses, regression analyses and other correlational analyses. Gallup scientists continued to study the core concepts that differentiated successful from less successful work units and the expressions that best captured those concepts. In 1997, the criterion-related studies were combined into a meta-analysis to study the relationship of employee satisfaction and engagement (as measured by the Q^{12}) to business/work unit profitability, productivity, employee retention and customer satisfaction/loyalty across 1,135 business/work units (Harter & Creglow, 1997). Meta-analysis also enabled researchers to study the generalizability of the relationship between engagement and outcomes. Results of this confirmatory analysis revealed substantial criterion-related validity for each of the Q^{12} items.

As criterion-related validity studies are ongoing, the meta-analysis was updated in 1998 (Harter & Creglow, 1998) and included 2,528 business/work units; in 2000 (Harter & Schmidt, 2000), when it included 7,939 business/work units; in 2002 (Harter & Schmidt, 2002), when it included 10,885 business/work units; in 2003 (Harter, Schmidt, & Killham, 2003), when it included 13,751 business/work units; in 2006 (Harter, Schmidt, Killham, & Asplund, 2006), when it included 23,910 business/work units; in 2009 (Harter, Schmidt, Killham, & Agrawal, 2009), when it included 32,394 business/work units; in 2013 (Harter, Schmidt, Agrawal, & Plowman, 2013), when it included 49,928 business/work units; and in 2016 (Harter, Schmidt, Agrawal, Plowman, & Blue, 2016), when it included 82,248 business/work units. This report provides the 10th published iteration of Gallup's Q^{12} meta-analysis on the relationship between employee engagement and performance.

As with the 2016 report, this report expands the number of business/work units and increases the total composition of different industries and countries studied. It also includes two new outcome variables: wellbeing and organizational citizenship.

Since its final wording and order were completed in 1998, the Q^{12} has been administered to more than 43 million employees in 212 different countries or territories and in 74 languages. Additionally, a series of studies was conducted to examine the cross-cultural properties of the instrument (Harter & Agrawal, 2011).

Introduction to the Study

The quality of an organization's human resources is perhaps the leading indicator of its growth and sustainability. The attainment of a workplace with high-caliber employees starts with the selection of the right people for the right jobs. Numerous studies have documented the utility of valid selection instruments and systems in the selection of the right people

(Schmidt, Hunter, McKenzie, & Muldrow, 1979; Hunter & Schmidt, 1983; Huselid, 1995; Schmidt & Rader, 1999; Harter, Hayes, & Schmidt, 2004; Schmidt, Oh, & Shaffer, 2016).

After employees are hired, they make decisions and take actions every day that can affect the success of their organizations. Many of these decisions and actions are influenced by their own internal motivations and drives. One can also hypothesize that the way employees are treated and the way they treat one another can positively affect their actions — or can place their organizations at risk. For example, researchers have found positive relationships between general workplace attitudes and service intentions, customer perceptions (Schmit & Allscheid, 1995), and individual performance outcomes (Iaffaldano & Muchinsky, 1985). An updated meta-analysis has revealed a substantial relationship between individual job satisfaction and individual performance (Judge, Thoresen, Bono, & Patton, 2001). Additional and more recent research illustrates that individual job attitudes are a substantial predictor of individual employee effectiveness, defined by both performance and withdrawal behaviors and intentions (Harrison, Newman, & Roth, 2006; Mackay, Allen, & Landis, 2017). Both of these more recent studies found that employee engagement is best conceptualized as a higher order job attitudes construct. This is further reinforced by Newman, Harrison, Carpenter and Rariden (2016).

There is also evidence at the business or work unit level that employee attitudes relate to various organizational outcomes. Organization-level research has focused primarily on cross-sectional studies. Independent studies found relationships between employee attitudes and performance outcomes such as safety (Zohar, 1980, 2000), customer experiences (Schneider, Parkington, & Buxton, 1980; Ulrich, Halbrook, Meder, Stuchlik, & Thorpe, 1991; Schneider & Bowen, 1993; Schneider,

Ashworth, Higgs, & Carr, 1996; Schmit & Allscheid, 1995; Reynierse & Harker, 1992; Johnson, 1996; Wiley, 1991), financials (Denison, 1990; Schneider, 1991) and employee turnover (Ostroff, 1992). A study by Batt (2002) used multivariate analysis to examine the relationship between human resource practices (including employee participation in decision-making) and sales growth. Gallup has conducted large-scale meta-analyses, most recently studying 82,248 business and work units regarding the concurrent and predictive relationship of employee attitudes (satisfaction and engagement) with safety, customer attitudes, financials, employee retention, absenteeism, quality metrics and merchandise shrinkage (Harter et al., 2016; Harter et al., 2013; Harter et al., 2009; Harter et al., 2006; Harter et al., 2003; Harter, Schmidt, & Hayes, 2002; Harter & Schmidt, 2002; Harter & Schmidt, 2000; Harter & Creglow, 1998; Harter & Creglow, 1997). This meta-analysis, repeated across time, has found consistently that there are positive concurrent and predictive relationships between employee attitudes and various important business outcomes. It has also found that these relationships generalize across a wide range of situations (industries, business/work unit types and countries). Additional independent studies have found similar results (Whitman, Van Rooy, & Viswesvaran, 2010; Edmans, 2012). A recent meta-analysis of employee engagement data found somewhat stronger correlations between job attitudes and business performance during past economic recessions compared to nonrecession years (Harter, Schmidt, Agrawal, Plowman, & Blue, 2020). Like the studies of individual job attitudes, this study also found that the best predictor of overall business/work unit performance was a higher order job attitudes-engagement construct.

Even though it has been much more common to study employee opinion data at the individual level, studying data at the business or work unit level is critical because that is where the data are typically reported (because of confidentiality concerns, employee surveys are reported at a broader business or work unit level). In addition, business-unit-level research usually provides opportunities to establish links to outcomes that are directly relevant to most businesses — outcomes like customer loyalty, profitability, productivity, turnover, safety, merchandise shrinkage and quality variables that are often aggregated and reported at the business/work unit level.

Another advantage to reporting and studying data at the business/work unit level is that instrument item scores are of similar reliability to dimension scores for individual-level analysis. This is because at the business or work unit level, each item score is an average of many individuals' scores. This means that employee surveys reported at a business or work unit level can be more efficient or parsimonious in length because item-level measurement error is less of a concern. See Harter and Schmidt (2006) for a more complete discussion of job satisfaction research and the advantages of conducting unit-level analyses.

One potential problem with such business-unit-level studies is limited data as a result of a limited number of business/work units (the number of business/work units becomes the sample size) or limited access to outcome measures that one can compare across business/work units. For this reason, many of these studies are limited in statistical power. As such, results from individual studies may appear to conflict with one another. Meta-analysis techniques provide the opportunity to pool such studies together to obtain more precise estimates of the strength of effects and their generalizability.

This paper's purpose is to present the results of an updated meta-analysis of the relationship between employee workplace perceptions and business/work unit outcomes based on currently available data collected with Gallup clients. The focus of this study is on Gallup's Q^{12} instrument. The Q^{12} items — which were selected because of their importance at the business or work unit level — measure employee perceptions of the quality of people-related management practices in their business/work units.

Description of the Q^{12}

The development of the GWA (Q^{12}) was based on more than 30 years of accumulated quantitative and qualitative research. Its reliability, convergent validity and criterion-related validity have been extensively studied. It is an instrument validated through prior psychometric studies as well as practical considerations regarding its usefulness for managers in creating change in the workplace.

In designing the items included in the Q^{12}, researchers took into account that, from an actionability standpoint, there are two broad categories of employee survey items: those that are reflective measures of attitudinal outcomes (satisfaction, loyalty, pride, customer service perceptions and intent to stay with the company) and those that are formative measures of actionable issues that drive these outcomes. The Q^{12} measures the actionable issues for management — those predictive of attitudinal outcomes such as satisfaction, loyalty, pride and so on. On Gallup's standard Q^{12} instrument, after an overall satisfaction item are 12 items measuring issues we have found to be actionable (changeable) at the supervisor or manager level — items measuring perceptions of elements of the work situation, such as role clarity, resources, fit between abilities and requirements, receiving feedback, and feeling appreciated. The Q^{12} is a formative measure of "engagement conditions," each of which is a contributor to engagement through the measure of its causes.

The overall satisfaction item and Q¹² items are:

Q00. (Overall Satisfaction) On a 5-point scale, where 5 means extremely satisfied and 1 means extremely dissatisfied, how satisfied are you with (your company) as a place to work?

Q01. I know what is expected of me at work.

Q02. I have the materials and equipment I need to do my work right.

Q03. At work, I have the opportunity to do what I do best every day.

Q04. In the last seven days, I have received recognition or praise for doing good work.

Q05. My supervisor, or someone at work, seems to care about me as a person.

Q06. There is someone at work who encourages my development.

Q07. At work, my opinions seem to count.

Q08. The mission or purpose of my company makes me feel my job is important.

Q09. My associates or fellow employees are committed to doing quality work.

Q10. I have a best friend at work.

Q11. In the last six months, someone at work has talked to me about my progress.

Q12. This last year, I have had opportunities at work to learn and grow.

The current standard is to ask each employee (a census survey; median participation rate is 85%) to rate the Q^{12} statements using six response options, from 5 = strongly agree to 1 = strongly disagree, and the sixth response option — don't know/does not apply — is unscored. Because it is a satisfaction item, the first item (Q00) is scored on a satisfaction scale rather than on an agreement scale. Regression analyses (Harter et al., 2002) indicate that employee engagement accounts for nearly all of the performance-related variance (composite performance) accounted for by the overall satisfaction measure. Therefore, the focus of this report is on employee engagement, as measured by statements Q01-Q12.

While these items measure issues that the manager or supervisor can influence, only one item contains the word "supervisor." This is because it is realistic to assume that numerous people in the workplace can influence whether someone's expectations are clear, whether the employee feels cared about and so on. The manager's or supervisor's position, though, allows them to take the lead in establishing a culture that values behaviors that support these perceptions.

The following is a brief discussion of the conceptual relevance of each of the 13 items:

Q00. Overall satisfaction

The first item on the survey measures affective satisfaction on a scale from "extremely dissatisfied" to "extremely satisfied." It is an attitudinal outcome or direct reflective measure of how people feel about their organization. Given that it is a direct measure of affective satisfaction, on its own, it is difficult to act on the results of this item. Other issues, like those measured in the following 12 items, explain why people are satisfied and why they become engaged and produce outcomes.

Q01. Expectations

Defining and clarifying the outcomes that are to be achieved is perhaps the most basic of all employee needs and manager responsibilities. How these outcomes are defined and acted on will vary across business/work units, depending on the goals of the business/work unit.

Q02. Materials and equipment

Getting people what they need to do their work is important in maximizing efficiency, demonstrating to employees that their work is valued and showing that the company is supporting them in what they are asked to do. Great managers help employees see how their requests for materials and equipment connect to important organizational outcomes.

Q03. Opportunity to do what I do best

Helping people get into roles in which they can most fully use their inherent talents and strengths is the ongoing work of great managers. Learning about individual differences through experience and assessment can help the manager position people efficiently within and across roles and remove barriers to high performance.

Q04. Recognition for good work

Employees need constant feedback to know if what they are doing matters. Ongoing management challenges include understanding how each person prefers to be recognized, making recognition objective and real by basing it on performance, and recognizing employees frequently.

Q05. Someone at work cares about me

For each person, feeling cared about may mean something different. The best managers listen to individuals and respond to their unique needs. In addition, they find the connection between the needs of the individual and the needs of the organization.

Q06. Someone at work encourages my development

How employees are coached can influence how they perceive their future. If the manager is helping the employee improve as an individual by providing opportunities that are in sync with the employee's talents, both the employee and the company will profit.

Q07. Opinions count

Asking for the employee's input and considering that input can often lead to better decision-making. This is because employees are often closer than the manager is to many factors that affect the overall system, whether that is the customer or the products they are producing every day. In addition, when employees feel they are involved in decisions, they take greater ownership for the outcomes.

Q08. Mission or purpose

Great managers help people see not only the purpose of their work, but also how each person's work influences and relates to the purpose of the organization and its outcomes. Reminding employees of the big-picture effect of what they do each day is important, whether their work influences the customer, safety or the public.

Q09. Associates committed to quality

Managers can influence the extent to which employees respect one another by selecting conscientious employees, providing some common goals and metrics for quality, and increasing associates' frequency of opportunity for interaction.

Q10. Best friend at work

Managers vary in the extent to which they create opportunities for people at work to get to know one another and in how much they value close, trusting relationships at work. The best managers do not subscribe to the idea that there should be no close friendships at work; instead, they free people to get to know one another, which is a basic human need. This, then, can influence communication, trust and other outcomes.

Q11. Progress

Providing a structured time to discuss each employee's progress, achievements and goals is important for managers and employees. Great managers regularly meet with individuals, both to learn from them and to give them guidance. This give-and-take helps managers and employees make better decisions.

Q12. Opportunities to learn and grow

In addition to having a need to be recognized for doing good work, most employees need to know that they are improving and have opportunities to build their knowledge and skills. Great managers choose training that will benefit the individual and the organization.

More detailed discussion of the practical application of each Q^{12} item is provided in Wagner and Harter (2006) and in various articles posted on Gallup.com.

As a total instrument (sum or mean of items Q01-Q12), the Q^{12} has a Cronbach's alpha of 0.91 at the business/work unit level. The meta-analytic convergent validity of the equally weighted mean (or sum) of items Q01-Q12 (GrandMean) to the equally weighted mean (or sum) of additional items in longer surveys (measuring all known facets of job satisfaction and engagement) is 0.91. This provides evidence that the Q^{12}, as a composite measure, captures the general factor in longer employee surveys. Individual items correlate to their broader dimension true-score values, on average, at approximately 0.70. While the Q^{12} is a measure of actionable engagement conditions, its composite has high convergent validity with affective satisfaction and other direct measures of work engagement (see Harter and Schmidt, 2008, for further discussion of convergent and discriminant validity issues and the construct of "engagement").

As previously mentioned, this is the 10th published iteration of the Q^{12} business-unit-level meta-analysis. Compared with the previous meta-analysis, the current meta-analysis includes:

- a larger number of studies, business/work units and countries

- two new outcomes (wellbeing and organizational citizenship)

- more than double the number of business/work units with absenteeism data, 79% more business/work units with quality (defects) data, 43% more business/work units with turnover data, 23% more business/work units with customer loyalty/ engagement data and 17% more business/work units with productivity data

As such, this study provides a substantial update of new and recent data.

The coverage of research studies includes business/work units in 96 countries, including Australia; New Zealand; and countries in Asia, Europe, the Commonwealth of Independent States, Latin America, the Middle East, North America, Africa and the Caribbean. Fifty-two companies included in the current meta-analysis operate exclusively in countries outside the U.S.

This meta-analysis includes all available Gallup studies (whether published or unpublished) and has no risk of publication bias.

Meta-Analysis, Hypothesis, Methods and Results

Meta-Analysis

A meta-analysis is a statistical integration of data accumulated across many different studies. As such, it provides uniquely powerful information because it controls for measurement and sampling errors and other idiosyncrasies that distort the results of individual studies. A meta-analysis eliminates biases and provides an estimate of true validity or true relationship between two or more variables. Statistics typically calculated during meta-analyses also allow the researcher to explore the presence, or lack, of moderators of relationships.

More than 1,000 meta-analyses have been conducted in the psychological, educational, behavioral, medical and personnel selection fields. The research literature in the behavioral and social sciences fields includes a multitude of individual studies with apparently conflicting conclusions. Meta-analysis, however, allows the researcher to estimate the mean relationship between variables and make corrections for artifactual sources of variation in findings across studies. It provides a method by which researchers can determine whether validities and relationships generalize across various situations (e.g., across firms or geographical locations).

This paper will not provide a full review of meta-analysis. Rather, the authors encourage readers to consult the following sources for background information and detailed descriptions of the more recent meta-analytic methods: Schmidt and Hunter (2015); Schmidt (1992); Hunter and Schmidt (1990, 2004); Lipsey and Wilson (1993); Bangert-Drowns (1986); and Schmidt, Hunter, Pearlman and Rothstein-Hirsh (1985).

Hypothesis and Study Characteristics

The hypotheses examined for this meta-analysis were as follows:

Hypothesis 1

Business-unit-level employee engagement will have positive average correlations with the business/work unit outcomes of customer loyalty/ engagement, profitability, productivity, wellbeing and organizational citizenship, and negative correlations with turnover, safety incidents, absenteeism, shrinkage, patient safety incidents and quality (defects).

Hypothesis 2

The correlations between engagement and business/work unit outcomes will generalize across organizations for all business/work unit outcomes. That is, these correlations will not vary substantially across organizations. And in particular, there will be few, if any, organizations with zero correlations or those in the opposite direction from Hypothesis 1.

Gallup's inferential database includes 456 studies conducted as proprietary research for 276 independent organizations. In each Q^{12} study, data were aggregated at the business/work unit level and correlated with the following aggregate business/work unit performance measures:

- customer metrics (referred to as customer loyalty/engagement)

- profitability

- productivity

- turnover

- safety incidents

- absenteeism
- shrinkage
- patient safety incidents
- quality (defects)
- wellbeing
- organizational citizenship

That is, in these analyses, the unit of analysis was the business or work unit, not the individual employee.

Correlations (r values) were calculated, estimating the relationship of business/work unit average measures of employee engagement (the mean of the Q^{12} items) to each of these 11 general outcomes. Correlations were calculated across business/work units in each company, and these correlation coefficients were entered into a database. The researchers then calculated mean validities, standard deviations of validities and validity generalization statistics for each of the 11 business/work unit outcome measures.

As with previous meta-analyses, some of the studies were concurrent validity studies, where engagement and performance were measured in roughly the same time period or with engagement measurement slightly trailing behind the performance measurement (because engagement is relatively stable and a summation of the recent past, such studies are considered "concurrent"). Predictive validity studies involve measuring engagement at time 1 and performance at time 2. Predictive validity estimates were obtained for 47% of the organizations included in this meta-analysis.

This paper does not directly address issues of causality, which are best addressed with meta-analytic longitudinal data, consideration of multiple variables and path analysis. Issues of causality are discussed and examined extensively in other sources (Harter, Schmidt, Asplund, Killham, & Agrawal, 2010). Findings of causal studies suggest that engagement and financial performance are reciprocally related, but that engagement is a stronger predictor of financial outcomes than the reverse. The relationship between engagement and financial performance appears to be mediated by its causal relationship with other outcomes such as customer perceptions and employee retention. That is, financial performance is a downstream outcome that is influenced by the effect of engagement on shorter-term outcomes such as customer perceptions and employee retention.

Studies for the current meta-analysis were selected so that each organization was represented once in each analysis. For several organizations, multiple studies were conducted. To include the best possible information for each organization represented in the study, some basic rules were used. If two concurrent studies were conducted for the same client (where Q^{12} and outcome data were collected concurrently [i.e., in the same year]), then the weighted average effect sizes across the multiple studies were entered as the value for that organization. If an organization had a concurrent and a predictive study (where the Q^{12} was collected in year 1 and outcomes were tracked in year 2), then the effect sizes from the predictive study were entered. If an organization had multiple predictive studies, then the mean of the correlations in these studies was entered. If sample sizes varied substantially in repeated studies for an organization, the study with the largest sample size was used.

- For 107 organizations, there were studies that examined the relationship between business/work unit employee perceptions and customer perceptions. Customer perceptions included customer metrics, patient metrics and student ratings of teachers. These metrics included measures of loyalty, satisfaction, service excellence, customer evaluation of quality of claims, net promoter scores and engagement. The largest representation of studies included loyalty metrics (e.g., likelihood to recommend/net promoter or repeat business), so we refer to customer metrics as customer loyalty/engagement in this study. Instruments varied from study to study. The general index of customer loyalty was an average score of the items included in each measure. A growing number of studies include "customer engagement" as the metric of choice, which measures the emotional connection between the customers and the organization that serves them. For more information on the interaction of employee and customer engagement, see Fleming, Coffman and Harter (2005), and Harter, Asplund and Fleming (2004).

- Profitability studies were available for 90 organizations. The definition of profitability typically was a percentage profit of revenue (sales). In several companies, the researchers used — as the best measure of profit — a difference score from the prior year or a difference from a budgeted amount because it represented a more accurate measure of each unit's relative performance. As such, a control for opportunity (location) was used when profitability figures were deemed less comparable from one unit to the next. For example, a difference variable involved dividing profit by revenue for a business/work unit and then subtracting a budgeted percentage from this percentage. Or, more explicitly, in some cases, a partial correlation (r value) was calculated, controlling for location variables when they were deemed to be relevant to accurate comparison of business/work units. In every case, profitability variables were measures of margin, and productivity variables (which follow) were measures of amount produced.

- Productivity studies were available for 162 organizations. Measures of business/work unit productivity consisted of one of the following: financials (e.g., revenue/sales dollars per person or patient), quantity produced (production volume), enrollments in programs, hours/labor costs to budget, cross-sells, performance ratings or student achievement scores (for three education organizations). In a few cases, this was a dichotomous variable (top-performing business/work units = 2; less successful units = 1). The majority of variables included as "productivity" were financial measures of sales or revenue, or growth in sales or revenue. As with profitability, in many cases, it was necessary for the researchers to compare financial results with a performance goal or prior-year figure to control for the differential business opportunity because of the location of business/work units, or to explicitly calculate a partial correlation (r value). Variables included in this category could best be summarized as financial metrics, evaluations or production records.

- Turnover data were available for 128 organizations. The turnover measure was the annualized percentage of employee turnover for each business/work unit. In most cases, voluntary turnover was reported and used in the analyses.

- Safety data were available for 59 organizations. Safety measures included lost workday/time incident rate, percentage of workdays lost as a result of incidents or workers' compensation claims (incidents and costs), number of incidents, or incident rates.

- Absenteeism data were included for 37 organizations. Absenteeism measures included the average number of days missed per person for each business/work unit divided by the total days available for work. The measures of absenteeism included sick days or hours absent or total days absent.

- Eleven organizations provided measures of shrinkage. Shrinkage is defined as the dollar amount of unaccounted-for lost merchandise, which could be the result of employee theft, customer theft or lost merchandise. Given the varying size of locations, shrinkage was calculated as a percentage of total revenue or a difference from an expected target.

- Ten healthcare organizations provided measures of patient safety. Patient safety incident measures varied from patient fall counts (percentages of total patients), medical error and infection rates, and risk-adjusted mortality rates.

- Twenty organizations provided measures of quality. For most organizations, quality was measured through records of defects such as unsalable/returned items/quality shutdowns/scrap/operational efficiency/rejections per inspection rate (in manufacturing), forced outages (in utilities), disciplinary actions, deposit accuracy (financial) and other quality scores. Because the majority of quality metrics were measures of defects (where higher figures meant worse performance), measures of efficiency and quality scores were reverse coded so that all variables carried the same inferential interpretation.

- Wellbeing measures were collected by 12 organizations. In all studies, the wellbeing measure was the Cantril Self-Anchoring Striving Scale. The scale measures respondents' life evaluation on the 0-10 ladder of life "at this time" and anticipated life evaluation "about five years from now." The scale is anchored from "best possible life" (10) to "worst possible life" (0).

- Organizational citizenship measures were available for two organizations. These measures consisted of the percentage of participation and enrollment in company-sponsored activities that are intended to benefit employees, such as conferences and programs. Wellness conferences and 401(k) enrollment are examples from the two organizations that provided data.

The overall study involved 2,708,538 independent employee responses to surveys and 112,312 independent business/work units in 276 organizations, with an average of 24 employees per business/work unit and 407 business/work units per organization. We conducted 456 research studies across the 276 organizations.

Table 1 provides a summary of industries included in this meta-analysis. It is evident that there is considerable variation in the industry types represented, as organizations from 54 industries provided studies. Each of the general government industry classifications (via SIC codes) is represented, with the largest number of organizations represented in services, retail, manufacturing and finance industries. The largest numbers of business/work units are in the services, finance and retail industries. Specific subindustry frequencies are detailed in Table 1.

Table 1: Summary of Industries

Industry Type	Number of Organizations	Number of Business/ Work Units	Number of Respondents
FINANCE			
Commercial Banking	6	3,132	21,435
Credit	2	59	581
Depository	21	16,230	176,430
Insurance	10	7,837	79,464
Mortgage	1	27	985
Nondepository	1	94	2,038
Security	4	797	25,833
Transactions	1	73	1,530
MANUFACTURING			
Aircraft	1	3,411	37,616
Apparel	1	16	111
Automobiles	1	30	1,453
Building Materials	1	8	1,335
Chemicals	1	928	8,203
Computers and Electronics	3	239	27,002
Consumer Goods	5	289	13,098
Food	7	3,116	91,337
Glass	1	5	1,349
Industrial Equipment	1	89	639
Instrument	8	535	5,848
Miscellaneous	4	924	22,481
Paper	2	753	27,025
Pharmaceutical	5	4,103	39,575
Plastics	1	133	938
Printing	2	35	716
Ship Building	3	882	134,297

Table 1: Summary of Industries (continued)

Industry Type	Number of Organizations	Number of Business/ Work Units	Number of Respondents
MATERIALS AND CONSTRUCTION			
Materials and Construction	4	1,270	29,932
RETAIL			
Automotive	4	261	13,614
Building Materials	3	1,158	65,001
Clothes	4	1,055	28,937
Department Stores	2	752	6,594
Eating	8	1,296	57,104
Electronics	6	1,483	104,273
Entertainment	1	106	1,051
Food	6	7,101	344,559
Industrial Equipment	1	11	484
Miscellaneous	12	4,170	158,264
Pharmaceutical	2	8,288	171,463
SERVICES			
Agricultural	1	7	635
Business	4	1,258	16,162
Education	10	1,259	22,142
Government	7	11,127	213,631
Health	68	14,807	326,483
Hospitality	11	1,241	190,473
Nursing Home	2	508	28,768
Personal Services	1	424	3,226
Real Estate	4	321	7,924
Recreation	2	49	1,969
Social Services	4	1,621	28,602

Table 1: Summary of Industries (continued)

Industry Type	Number of Organizations	Number of Business/ Work Units	Number of Respondents
TRANSPORTATION/PUBLIC UTILITIES			
Airlines	1	111	2,293
Communications	7	4,234	46,784
Delivery Services	1	639	53,151
Electric, Gas and Sanitary Services	5	3,183	28,887
Nonhazardous Waste Disposal	1	727	28,600
Trucking	1	100	6,213
TOTAL			
Finance	46	28,249	308,296
Manufacturing	47	15,496	413,023
Materials and Construction	4	1,270	29,932
Retail	49	25,681	951,344
Services	114	32,622	840,015
Transportation/Public Utilities	16	8,994	165,928
TOTAL	**276**	**112,312**	**2,708,538**

Table 2 provides a summary of the business/work unit types included in this meta-analysis. There is considerable variation in the types of business/work units, ranging from stores to plants/mills to departments to schools. Overall, 22 different types of business/work units are represented; the largest number of organizations had studies of workgroups (teams), stores or bank branches. Likewise, workgroups, stores and bank branches have the highest proportional representation of business/work units.

Table 2: Summary of Business/Work Unit Types

Business/Work Unit Type	Number of Organizations	Number of Business/ Work Units	Number of Respondents
Bank Branch	20	18,118	196,481
Call Center	7	1,240	22,076
Child Care Center	1	1,562	25,661
Cost Center	16	3,675	76,758
Country	1	26	2,618
Dealership	7	423	16,940
Department	12	1,553	33,132
Division	3	714	134,703
Facility	2	1,080	55,182
Hospital	7	800	69,028
Hotel	9	846	182,953
Location	14	11,414	269,829
Mall	2	216	3,790
Patient Care Unit	8	2,825	52,703
Plant/Mill	8	2,106	100,871
Region	2	113	13,520
Restaurant	6	588	34,866
Sales Division	6	391	21,722
Sales Team	6	420	27,543
School	6	409	10,496
Store	37	24,124	893,781
Workgroup (Team)	96	39,669	463,885
TOTAL	276	112,312	2,708,538

Meta-Analytic Methods Used

Analyses included weighted average estimates of true validity; estimates of standard deviation of validities; and corrections made for sampling error, measurement error in the dependent variables, and range variation and restriction in the independent variable (Q^{12} GrandMean) for these validities. An additional analysis was conducted, correcting for independent-variable measurement error. The most basic form of meta-analysis corrects variance estimates only for sampling error. Other corrections recommended by Hunter and Schmidt (1990, 2004) and Schmidt and Hunter (2015) include correction for measurement and statistical artifacts such as range restriction and measurement error in the performance variables gathered. The sections that follow provide the definitions of the previously mentioned procedures.

Gallup researchers gathered performance-variable data for multiple time periods to calculate the reliabilities of the performance measures. Because these multiple measures were not available for each study, the researchers used artifact distributions meta-analysis methods (Hunter & Schmidt, 1990, pp. 158-197; Hunter & Schmidt, 2004) to correct for measurement error in the performance variables. The artifact distributions were based on test-retest reliabilities, where they were available, from various studies. The procedure followed for calculation of business/work unit outcome-measure reliabilities was consistent with scenario 23 in Schmidt and Hunter (1996). To take into account that some change in outcomes (stability) is a function of real change, test-retest reliabilities were calculated using the following formula:

$$(r_{12} \times r_{23})/r_{13}$$

Where r_{12} is the correlation of the outcome measured at time 1 with the same outcome measured at time 2, r_{23} is the correlation of the outcome measured at time 2 with the outcome measured at time 3, and r_{13} is the correlation of the outcome measured at time 1 with the outcome measured at time 3.

The above formula factors out real change (which is more likely to occur from time 1 to 3 than from time 1 to 2 or 2 to 3) from random changes in business/work unit results caused by measurement error, data collection errors, sampling errors (primarily in customer and quality measures) and uncontrollable fluctuations in outcome measures. Some estimates were available for quarterly data, some for semiannual data and others for annual data. The average time period in artifact distributions used for this meta-analysis was consistent with the average time period across studies for each criterion type. See Appendix A for a listing of the reliabilities used in the corrections for measurement error. Artifact distributions for reliability were collected for customer loyalty/engagement, profitability, productivity, turnover, safety incidents and quality (defects) measures. They were not collected for absenteeism, shrinkage, patient safety incidents, wellbeing and organizational citizenship because they were not available at the time of this study. Therefore, the assumed reliability for these outcomes was 1.00, resulting in downwardly biased true validity estimates (the estimates of validity reported here are lower than reality). Artifact distributions for these variables will be added as they become available in the future.

It could be argued that, because the independent variable (employee engagement as measured by the Q^{12}) is used in practice to predict outcomes, the practitioner must live with the reliability of the instrument being used. However, correcting for measurement error in the independent variable answers the theoretical question of how the actual constructs (true scores) relate to each other. Therefore, we present analyses both before and after correcting for independent variable reliability. Appendix B presents the distributions of reliabilities for the GrandMean of Q^{12}. These values were computed in the same manner as were those for the performance outcomes.

In correcting for range variation and range restriction, there are fundamental theoretical questions that need to be considered relating to whether such correction is necessary. In personnel selection, validities are routinely corrected for range restriction because in selecting applicants for jobs, those scoring highest on the predictor are typically selected. This results in explicit range restriction that biases observed correlations downward (i.e., attenuation). But in the employee satisfaction and engagement arena, one could argue that there is no explicit range restriction because we are studying results as they exist in the workplace. Business/work units are not selected based on scores on the predictor (Q^{12} scores).

However, we have observed that there is variation across companies in standard deviations of engagement. One hypothesis for why this variation occurs is that companies vary in how they encourage employee satisfaction and engagement initiatives and in how they have or have not developed a common set of values and a common culture. Therefore, the standard deviation of the population of business/work units across organizations studied will be greater than the standard deviation within the typical company. This variation in standard deviations across companies can be thought of as indirect range restriction (as opposed to direct range restriction). Improved indirect range restriction corrections have been incorporated into this meta-analysis (Hunter, Schmidt, & Le, 2006).

Since the development of the Q^{12}, Gallup has collected descriptive data on more than 43 million respondents, 5.1 million business/work units and 5,076 organizations. This accumulation of data indicates that the standard deviation within a given company is approximately four-fifths the standard deviation in the population of all business/work units. In addition, the ratio of standard deviation for a given organization relative to the population value varies from organization to organization. Therefore, if one goal is to estimate the effect size in the population of all business/work units (arguably a theoretically important issue), then correction should be made based on such available data. In the observed data, correlations are attenuated for organizations with less variability across business/work units than the population average and vice versa. As such, variability in standard deviations across organizations will create variability in observed correlations and is therefore an artifact that can be corrected for in interpreting the generalizability of validities. Appendixes in Harter and Schmidt (2000) provide artifact distributions for range-restriction/variation corrections used for meta-analysis. These artifact distributions were updated substantially in 2009 and have again been updated for this meta-analysis. We have included a randomly selected 100 organizations in our current artifact distributions. Because of the large size of these tables, they are not included in this report. They resemble those reported in the earlier study but include a larger number of entries.

The following excerpt provides an overview of meta-analysis conducted using artifact distributions:

In any given meta-analysis, there may be several artifacts for which artifact information is only sporadically available. For example, suppose measurement error and range restriction are the only relevant artifacts beyond sampling error. In such a case, the typical artifact distribution-based meta-analysis is conducted in three stages:

1. Information is compiled on four distributions: the distribution of the observed correlations, the distribution of the reliability of the independent variable, the distribution of the reliability of the dependent variable and the distribution of the range departure. There are then four means and four variances compiled from the set of studies, with each study providing whatever information it contains.

2. The distribution of observed correlations is corrected for sampling error.

3. The distribution corrected for sampling error is then corrected for error of measurement and range variation (Hunter & Schmidt, 1990, pp. 158-159; Hunter & Schmidt, 2004).

In this study, statistics are calculated and reported at each level of analysis, starting with the observed correlations and then correcting for sampling error, measurement error and, finally, range variation. Both within-organization range-variation corrections (to correct validity generalization estimates) and between-organization range-restriction corrections (to correct for differences in variation across organizations) were made. Between-organization range-restriction corrections are relevant in understanding how engagement relates to performance across the business/work units of all organizations. As alluded to, we have applied the indirect range-restriction correction procedure to this meta-analysis (Hunter et al., 2006).

The meta-analysis includes an estimate of the mean sample-size-weighted validity and the variance across the correlations — again weighting each validity by its sample size. The amount of variance predicted for weighted correlations based on sampling error was also computed. The following is the formula to calculate variance expected from sampling error in "bare bones" meta-analyses, using the Hunter et al. (2006) technique referred to previously:

$$s_e^2 = (1 - \bar{r}^2)^2 / (\overline{N} - 1)$$

Residual standard deviations were calculated by subtracting the amount of variance due to sampling error, the amount of variance due to study differences in measurement error in the dependent variable, and the amount of variance due to study differences in range variation from the observed variance. To estimate the true validity of standard deviations, the residual standard deviation was adjusted for bias due to mean unreliability and mean range restriction. The amount of variance due to sampling error, measurement error and range variation was divided by the observed variance to calculate the total percentage variance accounted for. Generalizability is generally assumed if a high percentage (such as 75%) of the variance in validities across studies is due to sampling error and other artifacts, or if the 90% credibility value (10th percentile of the distribution of true validities) is in the hypothesized direction. As in Harter et al. (2002), Harter et al. (2006), Harter et al. (2009), Harter et al. (2013) and Harter et al. (2016), we calculated the correlation of engagement to composite performance. This calculation assumes that managers are managing toward multiple outcomes simultaneously and that each outcome occupies some space in the overall evaluation of performance. To calculate the correlation to the composite index of performance, we used the Mosier (1943) formula to determine the reliability of the composite measure (as described in Harter et al., 2002), using reliability distributions and intercorrelations of the outcome measures. Patient safety was combined with the more general "safety" category because patient safety is an industry-specific variable. The reliability of the composite metric is 0.91. Composite performance was measured as the equally weighted sum of customer loyalty/engagement, turnover (reverse scored as retention), safety (accidents and patient safety incidents reverse scored), absenteeism (reverse scored), shrinkage (reverse scored), financials (with profitability and productivity equally weighted) and quality (defects reverse scored). We also calculated composite performance as the equally weighted sum of the most direct outcomes of engagement — customer loyalty/engagement, turnover (reverse scored as retention), safety (accidents and patient safety incidents reverse scored), absenteeism (reverse scored), shrinkage (reverse scored) and quality (defects reverse scored). The reliability of this composite variable is 0.89. We did not include the newly added outcomes (wellbeing and organizational citizenship) to the composite performance estimates because we do not have estimates of their intercorrelation with the other outcome variables.

In our research, we used the Schmidt and Le (2004) meta-analysis package (the artifact distribution meta-analysis program with correction for indirect range restriction). The program package is described in Hunter and Schmidt (2004).

Results

The focus of analyses for this report is on the relationship between overall employee engagement (defined by an equally weighted GrandMean of Q^{12}) and a variety of outcomes. Table 3 provides the updated meta-analytic and validity generalization statistics for the relationship between employee engagement and performance for each of the 11 outcomes studied. Two forms of true validity estimation follow mean observed correlations and standard deviations. The first corrects for range variation within organizations and dependent-variable measurement error. This range-variation correction places all organizations on the same basis in terms of variability of employee engagement across business/work units. These results can be viewed as estimating the relationships across business/work units within the average organization. The second corrects for range restriction across the population of business/work units and dependent-variable measurement error. Estimates that include the latter range-restriction correction apply to interpretations of effects in business/work units across organizations, as opposed to effects expected within a given organization. Because there is more variation in engagement for business/work units across organizations than there is within the average organization, effect sizes are higher when true validity estimates are calculated for business/work units across organizations.

For instance, observe the estimates relative to the customer loyalty/engagement criteria. Without the between-organization range-restriction correction (which is relevant to the effect within the typical organization), the true validity value of employee engagement is 0.20 with a 90% credibility value (CV) of 0.13. With the between-organization range-restriction correction (which is relevant to business/work units across organizations), the true validity value of employee engagement is 0.29 with a 90% CV of 0.19.

As in the nine prior meta-analyses, findings here show high generalizability across organizations in the relationships between employee engagement and customer loyalty/engagement, profitability, productivity, turnover, safety, shrinkage and quality (defects) outcomes. And, for the two new outcomes (wellbeing and organizational citizenship), correlations are highly generalizable. Of the 11 outcomes, the correlation between employee engagement and wellbeing is the strongest, with a mean observed correlation of 0.56 and true validity of 0.72. Across the 11 outcomes, most of the variability in correlations across organizations was the result of sampling error, measurement error or range restriction in individual studies. All of the 90% credibility values are in the hypothesized direction. The largest variability in correlations across organizations was observed for the absenteeism outcome. This was mainly because one very large study was added with substantially stronger correlations than were observed in past studies. The mean true validity of the relationship between engagement and absenteeism was -0.38, and the 90% credibility value was -0.21, indicating wide generalizability in the direction of the relationship. The direction of the effect is predictable, but the size of effect across companies varies somewhat. Artifacts do not explain all of the variance in correlations of employee engagement and most outcomes, but they explain a high percentage of the variance in nearly all outcomes. This means that the Q^{12} measure of employee engagement effectively predicts these outcomes in the expected direction across organizations, including those in different industries and in different countries.

In summary, for the composite measure of engagement shown in Table 3, the strongest effects were found for wellbeing, patient safety incidents, absenteeism, quality (defects), customer loyalty/ engagement, safety incidents and productivity. Correlations were lower but highly generalizable for profitability, shrinkage, turnover and organizational citizenship.

Table 3: Meta-Analysis of Relationship Between Employee Engagement and Business/Work Unit Performance

	Customer Loyalty/ Engagement	Profitability	Productivity	Turnover	Safety Incidents	Absenteeism	Shrinkage	Patient Safety Incidents	Quality (Defects)	Wellbeing	Organizational Citizenship
Number of Business/Work Units	25,391	32,298	53,228	62,815	10,891	24,099	4,514	1,464	4,150	2,651	1,693
Number of r's	107	90	162	128	59	37	11	10	20	12	2
Mean Observed r	0.16	0.09	0.13	-0.08	-0.13	-0.27	-0.09	-0.43	-0.20	0.56	0.08
Observed SD	0.09	0.07	0.08	0.06	0.09	0.13	0.06	0.15	0.11	0.04	0.01
True Validity[1]	0.20	0.10	0.15	-0.12	-0.15	-0.27	-0.09	-0.43	-0.21	0.57	0.08
True Validity SD[1]	0.05	4.00	0.05	0.05	0.03	0.10	0.03	0.08	0.07	0	0
True Validity[2]	0.29	0.15	0.21	-0.18	-0.21	-0.38	-0.12	-0.56	-0.29	0.71	0.12
True Validity SD[2]	0.07	0.06	0.06	0.07	0.05	0.13	0.05	0.09	0.09	0	0
% Variance Accounted For — Sampling Error	50	58	46	49	73	8	60	23	40	114	708
% Variance Accounted For[1]	78	73	72	73	90	37	74	66	63	729	995
% Variance Accounted For[2]	78	73	72	73	90	37	74	66	64	810	995
90% CV[1]	0.13	0.05	0.09	-0.06	-0.11	-0.14	-0.05	-0.32	-0.12	0.57	0.08
90% CV[2]	0.19	0.08	0.13	-0.09	-0.16	-0.21	-0.06	-0.44	-0.18	0.71	0.12

r = correlation

SD = standard deviation

CV = credibility value

[1] Includes correction for range variation within organizations and dependent-variable measurement error

[2] Includes correction for range restriction across population of business/work units and dependent-variable measurement error

In the case of profitability, it is likely influenced indirectly by employee engagement and more directly by variables such as customer loyalty/engagement, productivity, turnover, safety, absenteeism, shrinkage, patient safety and quality. Remember, the productivity variable includes various measures of business/work unit productivity, the majority of which are sales data. Of the two financial variables included in the meta-analysis (sales and profit), engagement is more highly correlated with sales. This is probably because day-to-day employee engagement has an impact on customer perceptions, turnover, quality and other variables that relate to sales. In fact, this is what we have found empirically in our causal analyses (Harter et al., 2010). In the case of shrinkage, correlations may be somewhat lower because many factors influence merchandise shrinkage, including theft, attentiveness to inventory and damaged merchandise. The next section will explore the practical utility of the observed relationships.

As in Harter et al. (2002), we calculated the correlation of employee engagement to composite performance. As defined earlier, Table 4 provides the correlations and d-values for four analyses: the observed correlations; correction for dependent-variable measurement error; correction for dependent-variable measurement error and range restriction across companies; and correction for dependent-variable measurement error, range restriction and independent-variable measurement error (true score correlation).

As with previous meta-analyses, the effect sizes presented in Table 4 indicate substantial relationships between engagement and composite performance.

Business/work units in the top half on engagement within companies have 0.65 standard deviation units' higher composite performance compared with those in the bottom half on engagement.

Across companies, business/work units in the top half on engagement have 0.90 standard deviation units' higher composite performance compared with those in the bottom half on engagement.

After correcting for all available study artifacts (examining the true score relationship), business/work units in the top half on employee engagement have 1.12 standard deviation units' higher composite performance compared with those in the bottom half on engagement. This is the true score effect expected over time across all business/work units.

Table 4: Correlation of Employee Engagement to Composite Business/Work Unit Performance — All Outcomes

Analysis	Correlation of Engagement to Performance
Observed r	0.30
d	0.63
r corrected for dependent-variable measurement error	0.31
d	0.65
r corrected for dependent-variable measurement error and range restriction across companies	0.41
d	0.90
ρ corrected for dependent-variable measurement error, range restriction and independent-variable measurement error	0.49
δ	1.12

r = correlation
d = difference in standard deviation units
ρ = true score correlation
δ = true score difference in standard deviation units

As alluded to, some outcomes are the direct consequence of employee engagement (customer loyalty/engagement, turnover, safety, absenteeism, shrinkage and quality [defects]), and other outcomes are more of a downstream result of intermediary outcomes (sales and profit). For this reason, we have also calculated the composite correlation to short-term outcomes. Table 5 again indicates a substantial relationship between engagement and composite performance. Observed correlations and d-values are of the same magnitude as those reported in Table 4.

Table 5: Correlation of Employee Engagement to Composite Business/Work Unit Performance — Direct Outcomes (Customer Loyalty/Engagement, Turnover, Safety, Absenteeism, Shrinkage, Quality [Defects])

Analysis	Correlation of Engagement to Performance
Observed r	0.29
d	0.61
r corrected for dependent-variable measurement error	0.31
d	0.65
r corrected for dependent-variable measurement error and range restriction across companies	0.41
d	0.90
ρ corrected for dependent-variable measurement error, range restriction and independent-variable measurement error	0.49
δ	1.12

r = correlation
d = difference in standard deviation units
ρ = true score correlation
δ = true score difference in standard deviation units

Utility Analysis: Practicality of the Effects

In the past, studies of job satisfaction's relationship to performance have had limited analysis of the utility of the reported relationships. Correlations have often been discounted as trivial without an effort to understand the potential utility, in practice, of the relationships. The Q^{12} includes items that Gallup researchers have found to be changeable by the local manager and others within the business/work unit. As such, understanding the practical utility of potential changes is crucial.

The research literature includes a great deal of evidence that numerically small or moderate effects often translate into large practical effects (Abelson, 1985; Carver, 1975; Lipsey, 1990; Rosenthal & Rubin, 1982; Sechrest & Yeaton, 1982). As shown in Table 6, this is, in fact, the case here. Effect sizes referenced in this study are consistent with or above other practical effect sizes referenced in other reviews (Lipsey & Wilson, 1993).

A more intuitive method of displaying the practical value of an effect is that of binomial effect size displays, or BESDs (Rosenthal & Rubin, 1982; Grissom, 1994). BESDs typically depict the success rate of a treatment versus a control group as a percentage above the median on the outcome variable of interest.

BESDs can be applied to the results of this study. Table 6 shows the percentage of business/work units above the median on composite performance for high- and low-scoring business/work units on the employee engagement (Q^{12}) composite measure. True validity estimates (correcting for measurement error only in the dependent variable) were used for analysis of business/work units both within and across organizations.

One can see from Table 6 that there are meaningful differences between the top and bottom halves. The top half is defined as the average of business/work units scoring in the higher 50% on the Q^{12}, and business/work units scoring in the lower 50% constitute the bottom half. It is clear from Table 6 that management would learn a great deal more about success if it studied what was going on in top-half business/work units rather than bottom-half units.

With regard to composite business/work unit performance, business/work units in the top half on employee engagement have a 94% higher success rate in their own organization and a 145% higher success rate across business/work units in all companies studied. In other words, business/work units with high employee engagement nearly double their odds of above-average composite performance in their own organizations and increase their odds for above-average success across business/work units in all organizations by 2.45 times.

Table 6: BESDs for Employee Engagement and Outcomes

Employee Engagement	Business/Work Units Within Company	Business/Work Units Across Companies
	% Above Median Composite Performance (Total)	% Above Median Composite Performance (Total)
Top Half	66	71
Bottom Half	34	29
	% Above Median Composite Performance (Direct Outcomes)	% Above Median Composite Performance (Direct Outcomes)
Top Half	66	71
Bottom Half	34	29

To illustrate this further, Table 7 shows the probability of above-average performance for various levels of employee engagement. Business/work units at the highest level of employee engagement across all business/work units in Gallup's database have an 83% chance of having high (above average) composite performance. This compares with a 17% chance for those with the lowest level of employee engagement. So, it is possible to achieve high performance without high employee engagement, but the odds are substantially lower (in fact, nearly five times as low).

Table 7: Percentage of Business/Work Units Above the Company Median on Composite Performance (Customer Loyalty/Engagement, Profitability, Productivity, Turnover, Safety, Absenteeism, Shrinkage, Quality [Defects]) for Different Employee Engagement Percentiles

Employee Engagement Percentile	Percentage Above Company Median
Above 99th	83
95th	75
90th	70
80th	63
70th	58
60th	54
50th	50
40th	46
30th	42
20th	37
10th	30
5th	25
Below 1st	17

Other forms of expressing the practical meaning behind the effects from this study include utility analysis methods (Schmidt & Rauschenberger, 1986). Formulas have been derived for estimating the dollar-value increases in output as a result of improved employee selection. These formulas take into account the size of the effect (correlation), the variability in the outcome being studied and the difference in the independent variable (engagement in this case) and can be used in estimating the difference in performance outcomes at different levels in the distribution of Q^{12} scores. Previous studies (Harter et al., 2002; Harter & Schmidt, 2000) provided utility analysis examples, comparing differences in outcomes between the top and bottom quartiles on the Q^{12}. For companies included in the 2002 meta-analysis, it was typical to see differences between top and bottom engagement quartiles of 2 to 4 percentage points on customer loyalty/engagement, 1 to 4 points on profitability, hundreds of thousands of dollars on productivity figures per month, 4 to 19 points in turnover for low-turnover organizations and 14 to 51 points for high-turnover organizations.

Gallup researchers recently conducted utility analysis across multiple organizations with similar outcome metric types (an update of analyses presented in Harter et al., 2002, p. 275, Table 6). Comparing top-quartile with bottom-quartile engagement, business/work units resulted in median percent differences of:

- 10% in customer loyalty/engagement

- 23% in profitability

- 18% in productivity (sales)

- 14% in productivity (production records and evaluations)

- 18% in turnover for high-turnover organizations (those with more than 40% annualized turnover)

- 43% in turnover for low-turnover organizations (those with 40% or lower annualized turnover)

- 64% in safety incidents (accidents)

- 81% in absenteeism

- 28% in shrinkage (theft)

- 58% in patient safety incidents (mortality and falls)

- 41% in quality (defects)

- 66% in wellbeing (net thriving employees)

- 13% in organizational citizenship (participation)

The above differences and their utility in dollar terms should be calculated for each organization, given the organization's unique metrics, situation and distribution of outcomes across business/work units. The median estimates represent the midpoint in the distribution of utility analyses conducted across 426 studies based on organizational data with similar outcome types.

One can see that the above relationships are nontrivial if the business has many business/work units. The point of the utility analysis, consistent with the literature that has taken a serious look at utility, is that the relationship between employee engagement and organizational outcomes, even conservatively expressed, is meaningful from a practical perspective.

Discussion

Findings reported in this updated meta-analysis continue to provide large-scale cross-validation to prior meta-analyses conducted on the Q^{12} instrument. The present study expands the size of the meta-analytic database by 30,064 business/work units (an increase of 37%), as well as the number of countries and business/work units studied. The relationship between engagement and performance at the business/work unit level continues to be substantial and highly generalizable across companies. Differences in correlations across companies can be attributed mostly to study artifacts. For outcomes with sample sizes of 10,000 or more business/work units in 2016 (customer loyalty/engagement, profitability, productivity, turnover and absenteeism), the results of this updated meta-analysis are almost completely replicated. For the first four outcomes, differences in effect sizes from 2016 to 2020 ranged from 0.00 to 0.02, and evidence of generalizability remained substantial. For absenteeism, the effect size increased by 0.16, likely the result of one large study with a substantially higher effect size than the combination of other studies in the meta-analysis. But the direction of relationship between engagement and absenteeism was highly generalizable (90% credibility value of -0.21).

The size of this database gives us confidence in the direction of the true relationship between employee engagement and business outcomes and confidence in the size of the relationship, which can be helpful in calculating potential return on investment from performance management initiatives. The consistent findings across many iterations of meta-analysis also speak to the importance and relevance of workplace perceptions for businesses across different economic times and even amid massive changes in technology since 1997 when this study series began. As noted earlier, a recent meta-analysis found somewhat higher correlations of engagement and business results during past economic recessions (Harter et al., 2020).

The findings from this updated meta-analysis are important because they continue to reinforce that generalizable tools can be developed and used across different organizations with a high level of confidence that they elicit important performance-related information. The data from the present study provide further substantiation to the theory that doing what is best for employees does not have to contradict what is best for the business or organization. This concept is further reinforced in the present study with the newly reported strong relationship between employee engagement and wellbeing.

The strong association between engagement and wellbeing is supported by prior research. In worldwide samples, we have found consistent associations between engagement at work and life satisfaction, daily experiences and health (Gallup, 2010). A longitudinal study found that changes in engagement predicted changes in cholesterol and triglycerides (via blood samples) after controlling for demographics, health history and medication use (Harter, Canedy, & Stone, 2008). Even more recently, we have observed differences in momentary affect and cortisol when comparing engaged and disengaged employees (Harter & Stone, 2011). Consistent with the present study's finding of association between engagement and organizational citizenship, a previous study found that engagement at work predicts likelihood of involvement in organization-sponsored health programs (Agrawal & Harter, 2009). A previous meta-analysis found strong associations between job attitudes and citizenship behaviors (Whitman et al., 2010). Engagement has also been shown to be integral to perceptions of inclusiveness across diverse groups (Jones & Harter, 2004; Badal & Harter, 2014). All together, these studies suggest that the boundaries for the effect of an engaging workplace are quite wide.

It is also worth noting that, as Gallup consultants have educated managers and partnered with companies on change initiatives, organizations have experienced, on average, one-half standard deviation growth on employee engagement between the first and second year and often a full standard deviation growth and more after three or more years. An important element in the utility of any applied instrument and improvement process is the extent to which the variable under study can be changed. Our current evidence is that employee engagement is changeable and varies widely by business/work unit.

As we demonstrated in the utility analyses presented here and in other iterations of this analysis, the size of the effects observed has important practical implications, particularly given that engagement, as measured here, is quite changeable.

References

Abelson, R. P. (1985). A variance explanation paradox: When a little is a lot. *Psychological Bulletin*, 97(1), 129-133.

Agrawal, S., & Harter, J. K. (2009, October). *Employee engagement influences involvement in wellness programs*. Omaha, NE: Gallup.

Badal, S., & Harter, J. K. (2014). Gender diversity, business-unit engagement, & performance. *Journal of Leadership & Organizational Studies, 2*(4), 354-365.

Bangert-Drowns, R. L. (1986). Review of developments in meta-analytic method. *Psychological Bulletin, 99*(3), 388-399.

Batt, R. (2002). Managing customer services: Human resource practices, quit rates, and sales growth. *Academy of Management Journal, 45*(3), 587-597.

Carver, R. P. (1975). The Coleman Report: Using inappropriately designed achievement tests. *American Educational Research Journal, 12*(1), 77-86.

Denison, D. R. (1990). *Corporate culture and organizational effectiveness*. New York: John Wiley.

Edmans, A. (2012, November 1). The link between job satisfaction and firm value, with implications for corporate social responsibility. *Academy of Management Perspectives, 26*(4), 1-19.

Fleming, J. H., Coffman, C., & Harter, J. K. (2005, July-August). Manage your Human Sigma. *Harvard Business Review, 83*(7), 106-114.

Gallup (2010). *The state of the global workplace: A worldwide study of employee engagement and wellbeing*. Omaha, NE: Gallup.

Gallup, G. H. (1976, Winter). Human needs and satisfactions: A global survey. *Public Opinion Quarterly, 40*(4), 459-467.

Gallup, G., & Hill, E. (1960). *The secrets of long life*. New York: Bernard Geis.

The Gallup Organization (1993-1998). *Gallup Workplace Audit* (Copyright Registration Certificate TX-5 080 066). Washington, D.C.: U.S. Copyright Office.

Grissom, R. J. (1994). Probability of the superior outcome of one treatment over another. *Journal of Applied Psychology, 79*(2), 314-316.

Harrison, D. A., Newman, D. A., & Roth, P. L. (2006). How important are job attitudes? Meta-analytic comparisons of integrative behavioral outcomes and time sequences. *Academy of Management Journal, 49*(2), 305-325.

Harter, J. K., & Agrawal, S. (2011). *Cross-cultural analysis of Gallup's Q¹²
employee engagement instrument.* Omaha, NE: Gallup.

Harter, J. K., Asplund, J. W., & Fleming, J. H. (2004, August). *HumanSigma:
A meta-analysis of the relationship between employee engagement,
customer engagement and financial performance.* Omaha, NE: The Gallup Organization.

Harter, J. K., Canedy, J., & Stone, A. (2008). A longitudinal study of engagement at work and physiologic indicators of health. Presented at Work, Stress, & Health Conference. Washington, D.C.

Harter, J. K., & Creglow, A. (1997). *A meta-analysis and utility analysis of
the relationship between core GWA employee perceptions and business
outcomes.* Lincoln, NE: The Gallup Organization.

Harter, J. K., & Creglow, A. (1998, July). *A meta-analysis and utility analysis
of the relationship between core GWA employee perceptions and business
outcomes.* Lincoln, NE: The Gallup Organization.

Harter, J. K., Hayes, T. L., & Schmidt, F. L. (2004, January). *Meta-analytic
predictive validity of Gallup Selection Research Instruments (SRI).*
Omaha, NE: The Gallup Organization.

Harter, J. K., & Schmidt, F. L. (2000, March). *Validation of a performance-
related and actionable management tool: A meta-analysis and utility
analysis.* Princeton, NJ: The Gallup Organization.

Harter, J. K., & Schmidt, F. L. (2002, March). *Employee engagement,
satisfaction, and business-unit-level outcomes: A meta-analysis.* Lincoln,
NE: The Gallup Organization.

Harter, J. K., & Schmidt, F. L. (2006). Connecting employee satisfaction to business unit performance. In A. I. Kraut (Ed.), *Getting action from organizational surveys: New concepts, technologies, and applications* (pp. 33-52). San Francisco: Jossey-Bass.

Harter, J. K., & Schmidt, F. L. (2008). Conceptual versus empirical distinctions among constructs: Implications for discriminant validity. *Industrial and Organizational Psychology, 1*, 37-40.

Harter, J. K., Schmidt, F. L., Agrawal, S., & Plowman, S. K. (2013, February). *The relationship between engagement at work and organizational outcomes: 2012 $Q^{12®}$ meta-analysis.* Omaha, NE: Gallup.

Harter, J. K., Schmidt, F. L., Agrawal, S., Plowman, S. K., & Blue, A. (2016). *The relationship between engagement at work and organizational outcomes: 2016 $Q^{12®}$ meta-analysis: Ninth edition.* Omaha, NE: Gallup.

Harter, J. K., Schmidt, F. L., Agrawal, S., Plowman, S. K., & Blue, A. T. (2020). Increased business value for positive job attitudes during economic recessions: A meta-analysis and SEM analysis. *Human Performance, 33*(4), 307-330.

Harter, J. K., Schmidt, F. L., Asplund, J. W., Killham, E. A., & Agrawal, S. (2010). Causal impact of employee work perceptions on the bottom line of organizations. *Perspectives on Psychological Science, 5*(4), 378-389.

Harter, J. K., Schmidt, F. L., & Hayes, T. L. (2002). Business-unit-level relationship between employee satisfaction, employee engagement, and business outcomes: A meta-analysis. *Journal of Applied Psychology, 87*(2), 268-279.

Harter, J. K., Schmidt, F. L., & Killham, E. A. (2003, July). *Employee engagement, satisfaction, and business-unit-level outcomes: A meta-analysis.* Omaha, NE: The Gallup Organization.

Harter, J. K., Schmidt, F. L., Killham, E. A., & Agrawal, S. (2009). *Q^{12} meta-analysis.* Gallup. Omaha, NE.

Harter, J. K., Schmidt, F. L., Killham, E. A., & Asplund, J. W. (2006). *Q^{12} meta-analysis.* Gallup. Omaha, NE.

Harter, J. K., & Stone, A. A. (2012). Engaging and disengaging work conditions, momentary experiences and cortisol response. *Motivation and Emotion, 36*(2), 104-113.

Hunter, J. E., & Schmidt, F. L. (1983). Quantifying the effects of psychological interventions on employee job performance and work-force productivity. *American Psychologist, 38*(4), 473-478.

Hunter, J. E., & Schmidt, F. L. (1990). *Methods of meta-analysis: Correcting error and bias in research findings.* Newbury Park, CA: Sage.

Hunter, J. E., & Schmidt, F. L. (2004). *Methods of meta-analysis: Correcting error and bias in research findings* (2nd ed.). Newbury Park, CA: Sage.

Hunter, J. E., Schmidt, F. L., & Le, H. A. (2006). Implications of direct and indirect range restriction for meta-analysis methods and findings. *Journal of Applied Psychology, 91,* 594-612.

Huselid, M. A. (1995). The impact of human resource management practices on turnover, productivity, and corporate financial performance. *Academy of Management Journal, 38*(3), 635-672.

Iaffaldano, M. T., & Muchinsky, P. M. (1985). Job satisfaction and job performance: A meta-analysis. *Psychological Bulletin, 97*(2), 251-273.

Johnson, J. W. (1996). Linking employee perceptions of service climate to customer satisfaction. *Personnel Psychology, 49,* 831-851.

Jones, J. R., & Harter, J. K. (2004). Race effects on the employee engagement-turnover intention relationship. *Journal of Leadership & Organizational Studies, 11*(2), 78-87.

Judge, T. A., Thoresen, C. J., Bono, J. E., & Patton, G. K. (2001). The job satisfaction-job performance relationship: A qualitative and quantitative review. *Psychological Bulletin, 127*(3), 376-407.

Lipsey, M. W. (1990). *Design sensitivity: Statistical power for experimental research.* Newbury Park, CA: Sage.

Lipsey, M. W., & Wilson, D. B. (1993). The efficacy of psychological, educational, and behavioral treatment: Confirmation from meta-analysis. *American Psychologist, 48*(12), 1181-1209.

Mackay, M. M., Allen, J. A., & Landis, R. S. (2017). Investigating the incremental validity of employee engagement in the prediction of employee effectiveness: A meta-analytic path analysis. *Human Resource Management Review, 27*(1), 108-120.

Mosier, C. I. (1943). On the reliability of a weighted composite. *Psychometrika, 8*, 161-168.

Newman, D. A., Harrison, D. A., Carpenter, N. C., & Rariden, S. M. (2016). Construct mixology: Forming new management constructs by combining old ones. *The Academy of Management Annals, 10*(1), 943-995.

Ostroff, C. (1992). The relationship between satisfaction, attitudes, and performance: An organizational level analysis. *Journal of Applied Psychology, 77*(6), 963-974.

Reynierse, J. H., & Harker, J. B. (1992). Employee and customer perceptions of service in banks: Teller and customer service representative ratings. *Human Resource Planning, 15*(4), 31-46.

Rosenthal, R., & Rubin, D. B. (1982). A simple, general purpose display of magnitude of experimental effect. *Journal of Educational Psychology, 74*, 166-169.

Schmidt, F. L. (1992). What do data really mean? Research findings, meta-analysis, and cumulative knowledge in psychology. *American Psychologist, 47*(10), 1173-1181.

Schmidt, F. L., & Hunter, J. E. (1996). Measurement error in psychological research: Lessons from 26 research scenarios. *Psychological Methods, 1*(2), 199-223.

Schmidt, F. L., & Hunter, J. E. (2015). *Methods of meta-analysis: Correcting error and bias in research findings* (3rd ed.). Thousand Oaks, CA: Sage.

Schmidt, F. L., Hunter, J. E., McKenzie, R. C., & Muldrow, T. W. (1979). Impact of valid selection procedures on work-force productivity. *Journal of Applied Psychology, 64*(6), 609-626.

Schmidt, F. L., Hunter, J. E., Pearlman, K., & Rothstein-Hirsh, H. (1985). Forty questions about validity generalization and meta-analysis. *Personnel Psychology, 38*, 697-798.

Schmidt, F. L., & Le, H. A. (2004). Software for the Hunter-Schmidt meta-analysis methods. Iowa City, IA: Tippie College of Business, University of Iowa.

Schmidt, F. L., Oh, I. S., & Shaffer, J. A. (2016). The validity and utility of selection methods in personnel psychology: Practical and theoretical implications of 100 years of research findings. *Fox School of Business Research Paper.*

Schmidt, F. L., & Rader, M. (1999). Exploring the boundary conditions for interview validity: Meta-analytic validity findings for a new interview type. *Personnel Psychology, 52*, 445-464.

Schmidt, F. L., & Rauschenberger, J. (1986, April). *Utility analysis for practitioners.* Paper presented at the First Annual Conference of The Society for Industrial and Organizational Psychology, Chicago, IL.

Schmit, M. J., & Allscheid, S. P. (1995). Employee attitudes and customer satisfaction: Making theoretical and empirical connections. *Personnel Psychology, 48*, 521-536.

Schneider, B. (1991). Service quality and profits: Can you have your cake and eat it too? *Human Resource Planning, 14*(2), 151-157.

Schneider, B., Ashworth, S. D., Higgs, A. C., & Carr, L. (1996). Design, validity, and use of strategically focused employee attitude surveys. *Personnel Psychology, 49*(3), 695-705.

Schneider, B., & Bowen, D. E. (1993). The service organization: Human resources management is crucial. *Organizational Dynamics, 21*, 39-52.

Schneider, B., Parkington, J. J., & Buxton, V. M. (1980). Employee and customer perceptions of service in banks. *Administrative Science Quarterly, 25,* 252-267.

Sechrest, L., & Yeaton, W. H. (1982). Magnitudes of experimental effects in social science research. *Evaluation Review, 6*(5), 579-600.

Ulrich, D., Halbrook, R., Meder, D., Stuchlik, M., & Thorpe, S. (1991). Employee and customer attachment: Synergies for competitive advantage. *Human Resource Planning, 14*(2), 89-103.

Wagner, R., & Harter, J. K. (2006). *12: The elements of great managing.* New York: Gallup Press.

Whitman, D. S., Van Rooy, D. L., & Viswesvaran, C. (2010). Satisfaction, citizenship behaviors, and performance in work units: A meta-analysis of collective construct relations. *Personnel Psychology, 63*(1), 41-81.

Wiley, J. W. (1991). Customer satisfaction: A supportive work environment and its financial cost. *Human Resource Planning, 14*(2), 117-127.

Zohar, D. (1980). Safety climate in industrial organizations: Theoretical and applied implications. *Journal of Applied Psychology, 65*(1), 96-102.

Zohar, D. (2000). A group-level model of safety climate: Testing the effect of group climate on microaccidents in manufacturing jobs. *Journal of Applied Psychology, 85*(4), 587-596.

Appendix A: Reliabilities of Business/Work Unit Outcomes

Based on Schmidt & Hunter, 1996, scenario 23, page 219

Customer Loyalty/Engagement		Profitability		Productivity		Turnover		Safety		Quality (Defects)	
Reliability	Frequency	Reliability	Frequency	Reliability	Frequency	Reliability	Frequency	Reliability	Frequency	Reliability	Frequency
0.89	1	1.00	3	1.00	4	1.00	1	0.84	1	0.94	1
0.87	1	0.99	2	0.99	2	0.63	1	0.82	1		
0.86	1	0.94	1	0.92	2	0.62	1	0.66	1		
0.84	1	0.93	1	0.90	1	0.60	1	0.63	1		
0.75	1	0.91	1	0.62	1	0.39	1				
0.58	1	0.90	1	0.57	1	0.27	1				
0.53	2	0.89	2	0.34	1	0.25	1				
0.52	1	0.79	1			0.24	1				
0.51	1	0.57	1								
0.46	1	0.56	1								
0.41	1										
0.33	1										

Appendix B: Test-Retest Reliabilities of Employee Engagement

Based on Schmidt & Hunter, 1996, scenario 23, page 219

Engagement	
Reliability	Frequency
0.97	1
0.92	1
0.86	1
0.84	1
0.83	1
0.82	3
0.81	1
0.80	3
0.79	2
0.78	1
0.77	1
0.76	1
0.75	4
0.74	1
0.71	1
0.70	1
0.69	1
0.66	2
0.65	2
0.63	1
0.61	2
0.60	1
0.55	1
0.47	2
0.45	1
0.35	1
0.27	1

Appendix 5:
References and Notes

This book covers a wide range of research. For more details about Gallup's research and other studies referenced in the book's text, please see this expanded reference section.

For some references, we have included additional commentary.

Please note that any statistics not cited stem from Gallup research and studies.

Introduction: The Mood of the World

Case, A., & Deaton, A. (2020). *Deaths of despair and the future of capitalism.* Princeton University Press.

Chen, J. (2020). *Environmental, social, and governance (ESG) criteria.* Investopedia. https://www.investopedia.com/terms/e/environmental-social-and-governance-esg-criteria.asp

Department of Economic and Social Affairs: Sustainable Development. (n.d.). *The 17 goals.* United Nations. https://sdgs.un.org/goals

Rothwell, J. (2016). *No recovery: An analysis of long-term U.S. productivity decline.* Gallup and U.S. Council on Competitiveness.

Part 1: What Is Wellbeing?

What Is "The Best Possible Life"?

For perspective, in the late 1950s, only a mere 0.02% of Americans lived to be 95 or older — about 29,000 people at that time. As of the 2010 census, the percentage of Americans reaching age 95 or more has grown fivefold to 0.1% of the total U.S. population.

The average life expectancy in the U.S. at the time of Dr. Gallup's study was 70 years. In 2020, the average life expectancy was 79 years.

Berkman, L. F., Kawachi, I., & Glymour, M. M. (Eds.). (2014). *Social epidemiology*. Oxford University Press.

Berkman, L. F., & Syme, S. L. (1979). Social networks, host resistance, and mortality: A nine-year follow-up study of Alameda County residents. *American Journal of Epidemiology, 109*(2), 186-204.

Bosma, H., Marmot, M. G., Hemingway, H., Nicholson, A. C., Brunner, E., & Stansfeld, S. A. (1997). Low job control and risk of coronary heart disease in Whitehall II (prospective cohort) study. *BMJ, 314*(7080), 558-565.

Cappuccio, F. P., D'Elia, L., Strazzullo, P., & Miller, M. A. (2010). Sleep duration and all-cause mortality: A systematic review and meta-analysis of prospective studies. *Sleep, 33*(5), 585-592.

Chu, A. H. Y., Ng, S. H., Tan, C. S., Win, A. M., Koh, D., & Müller-Riemenschneider, F. (2016). A systematic review and meta-analysis of workplace intervention strategies to reduce sedentary time in white-collar workers. *Obesity Reviews, 17*(5), 467-481.

Diener, E. (2009). *Social indicators research series: vol. 37. The science of wellbeing: The collected works of Ed Diener*. Springer.

Diener, E., & Biswas-Diener, R. (2011). *Happiness: Unlocking the mysteries of psychological wealth*. Wiley-Blackwell.

Gallicchio, L., & Kalesan, B. (2009). Sleep duration and mortality: A systematic review and meta-analysis. *Journal of Sleep Research, 18*(2), 148-158.

Gallup, G. H., & Hill, E. (1960). *The secrets of long life.* Bernard Geis.

Goh, J., Pfeffer, J., & Zenios, S. A. (2016). The relationship between workplace stressors and mortality and health costs in the United States. *Management Science, 62*(2), 608-628.

Harter, J. K., & Agrawal, S. (April 2012). *Engagement at work: Working hours, flextime, vacation time, and well-being.* Gallup report.

Holt-Lunstad, J., Smith, T. B., & Layton, J. B. (2010). Social relationships and mortality risk: A meta-analytic review. *PLOS Medicine, 7*(7), e1000316.

Hutchinson, A. D., & Wilson, C. (2012). Improving nutrition and physical activity in the workplace: A meta-analysis of intervention studies. *Health Promotion International, 27*(2), 238-249.

Itani, O., Jike, M., Watanabe, N., & Kaneita, Y. (2017). Short sleep duration and health outcomes: A systematic review, meta-analysis, and meta-regression. *Sleep Medicine, 32*, 246-256.

Kelly, P., Kahlmeier, S., Götschi, T., Orsini, N., Richards, J., Roberts, N., Scarborough, P., & Foster, C. (2014). Systematic review and meta-analysis of reduction in all-cause mortality from walking and cycling and shape of dose response relationship. *International Journal of Behavioral Nutrition and Physical Activity, 11*(1), 132.

Kivimäki, M., Ferrie, J. E., Brunner, E., Head, J., Shipley, M. J., Vahtera, J., & Marmot, M. G. (2005). Justice at work and reduced risk of coronary heart disease among employees: The Whitehall II Study. *Archives of Internal Medicine, 165*(19), 2245-2251.

Kwok, C. S., Kontopantelis, E., Kuligowski, G., Gray, M., Muhyaldeen, A., Gale, C. P., Peat, G. M., Cleator, J., Chew-Graham, C., Loke, Y. K., & Mamas, M. A. (2018). Self-reported sleep duration and quality and cardiovascular disease and mortality: A dose-response meta-analysis. *Journal of the American Heart Association, 7*(15), e008552.

Li, J., Zhang, M., Loerbroks, A., Angerer, P., & Siegrist, J. (2014). Work stress and the risk of recurrent coronary heart disease events: A systematic review and meta-analysis. *International Journal of Occupational Medicine and Environmental Health*, 1-12.

Liu, M. Y., Li, N., Li, W. A., & Khan, H. (2017). Association between psychosocial stress and hypertension: A systematic review and meta-analysis. *Neurological Research, 39*(6), 573-580.

Loef, M., & Walach, H. (2012). The combined effects of healthy lifestyle behaviors on all cause mortality: A systematic review and meta-analysis. *Preventive Medicine, 55*(3), 163-170.

Martín-María, N., Miret, M., Caballero, F. F., Rico-Uribe, L. A., Steptoe, A., Chatterji, S., & Ayuso-Mateos, J. L. (2017). The impact of subjective well-being on mortality: A meta-analysis of longitudinal studies in the general population. *Psychosomatic Medicine, 79*(5), 565-575.

Public Opinion Surveys, Inc. (1959, May 8). *Who lives to be 95 and older? A study of 402 Americans 95 years of age and over.* Princeton, NJ.

Rath, T., & Harter, J. (2010). *Wellbeing: The five essential elements.* Gallup Press.

Richardson, S., Shaffer, J. A., Falzon, L., Krupka, D., Davidson, K. W., & Edmondson, D. (2012). Meta-analysis of perceived stress and its association with incident coronary heart disease. *The American Journal of Cardiology, 110*(12), 1711-1716.

Roelfs, D. J., Shor, E., Davidson, K. W., & Schwartz, J. E. (2011). Losing life and livelihood: A systematic review and meta-analysis of unemployment and all-cause mortality. *Social Science & Medicine, 72*(6), 840-854.

Seidelmann, S. B., Claggett, B., Cheng, S., Henglin, M., Shah, A., Steffen, L. M., Folsom, A. R., Rimm, E. B., Willett, W. C., & Solomon, S. D. (2018). Dietary carbohydrate intake and mortality: A prospective cohort study and meta-analysis. *Lancet Public Health, 3*(9), e419-e428.

Wang, Y. H., Li, J. Q., Shi, J. F., Que, J. Y., Liu, J. J., Lappin, J. M., Leung, J., Ravindran, A. V., Chen, W. Q., Qiao, Y. L., Shi, J., Lu, L., & Bao, Y. P. (2019). Depression and anxiety in relation to cancer incidence and mortality: A systematic review and meta-analysis of cohort studies. *Molecular Psychiatry, 25*(7), 1487-1499.

Yin, J., Jin, X., Shan, Z., Li, S., Huang, H., Li, P., Peng, X., Peng, Z., Yu, K., Bao, W., Yang, W., Chen, X., & Liu, L. (2017). Relationship of sleep duration with all-cause mortality and cardiovascular events: A systematic review and dose-response meta-analysis of prospective cohort studies. *Journal of the American Heart Association, 6*(9), e005947.

Net Thriving: The Other Stock Price

Based on a global sample of 51,741 respondents in 2019, 30% of employees worldwide were thriving in their overall lives, 20% were engaged in their work, and 9% of employees were both thriving *and* engaged at work.

Cantril, H. (1965). *The pattern of human concerns.* Rutgers University Press.

Cropanzano, R., & Wright, T. A. (1999). A 5-year study of change in the relationship between well-being and job performance. *Consulting Psychology Journal: Practice and Research, 51*(4), 252-265.

Deaton, A. (2008). Income, health, and well-being around the world: Evidence from the Gallup World Poll. *Journal of Economic Perspectives, 22*(2), 53-72.

Diener, E., Kahneman, D., Arora, R., Harter, J., & Tov, W. (2009). Income's differential influence on judgments of life versus affective well-being. In *Assessing Well-Being* (pp. 233-246). Springer.

Diener, E., Ng, W., Harter, J., & Arora, R. (2010). Wealth and happiness across the world: Material prosperity predicts life evaluation, whereas psychosocial prosperity predicts positive feeling. *Journal of Personality and Social Psychology, 99*(1), 52-61.

Erdogan, B., Bauer, T. N., Truxillo, D. M., & Mansfield, L. R. (2012). Whistle while you work: A review of the life satisfaction literature. *Journal of Management, 38*(4), 1038-1083.

Ford, M. T., Cerasoli, C. P., Higgins, J. A., & Decesare, A. L. (2011). Relationships between psychological, physical, and behavioural health and work performance: A review and meta-analysis. *Work & Stress, 25*(3), 185-204.

Harter, J. (2020, June 26). *If your employees aren't thriving, your business is struggling.* Gallup. https://www.gallup.com/workplace/313067/employees-aren-thriving-business-struggling.aspx

Kahneman, D., & Deaton, A. (2010). High income improves evaluation of life but not emotional well-being. *PNAS, 107*(38), 16489-16493.

O'Boyle, E., & Harter, J. (2014, May 13). *Why your workplace wellness program isn't working.* Gallup. https://www.gallup.com/workplace/236531/why-workplace-wellness-program-isn-working.aspx

Oswald, A. J., Proto, E., & Sgroi, D. (2015). Happiness and productivity. *Journal of Labor Economics, 33*(4), 789-822.

Salgado, J. F., & Moscoso, S. (2020). *Subjective well-being and job performance relationships across the world: Comprehensive meta-analysis and cross-cultural evidence.* [Unpublished manuscript]. University of Santiago de Compostela, Santiago de Compostela, Spain.

Understanding how Gallup uses the Cantril Scale: Development of the "thriving, struggling, suffering" categories. (n.d.). Gallup. https://news.gallup.com/poll/122453/Understanding-Gallup-Uses-Cantril-Scale.aspx

The Five Elements of Wellbeing

Agrawal, S. & Harter, J. K. (2011). *A worldwide study of the relationship between five wellbeing elements and life evaluation, daily experiences, health, and giving: A meta-analysis.* Gallup Technical Report.

Craig, H. (2020). *The philosophy of happiness in life (+ Aristotle's view).* PositivePsychology.com. https://positivepsychology.com/philosophy-of-happiness/

Diener, E., Ng, W., Harter, J., & Arora, R. (2010). Wealth and happiness across the world: Material prosperity predicts life evaluation, whereas psychosocial prosperity predicts positive feeling. *Journal of Personality and Social Psychology, 99*(1), 52-61.

Human needs and satisfactions: A global survey. (1977). The Charles F. Kettering Foundation and Gallup International Research Institutes. Research report.

Jones, J. M. (2020, June 22). *In U.S., negative emotions surged, then declined in June.* Gallup. https://news.gallup.com/poll/312872/negative-emotions-surged-declined-june.aspx

Kahneman, D. (2011). *Thinking, fast and slow.* Farrar, Straus and Giroux.

Kahneman, D., & Deaton, A. (2010). High income improves evaluation of life but not emotional well-being. *PNAS, 107*(38), 16489-16493.

Rath, T., & Harter, J. (2010). *Wellbeing: The five essential elements.* Gallup Press.

Stone, A. A., Schneider, S., & Harter, J. K. (2012). Day-of-week mood patterns in the United States: On the existence of 'blue Monday,' 'thank God it's Friday' and weekend effects. *The Journal of Positive Psychology, 7*(4), 306-314.

Witters, D., & Agrawal, S. (2020, August 16). *After record drop, U.S. life ratings partially rebound.* Gallup. https://news.gallup.com/poll/315614/record-drop-life-ratings-partially-rebound.aspx

Witters, D., & Harter, J. (2020, May 8). *Worry and stress fuel record drop in U.S. life satisfaction.* Gallup. https://news.gallup.com/poll/310250/worry-stress-fuel-record-drop-life-satisfaction.aspx

Part 2: Your Workplace's Wellbeing Opportunities

Key Points About the Wellbeing Elements

Abbe, A., Tkach, C., & Lyubomirsky, S. (2003). The art of living by dispositionally happy people. *Journal of Happiness Studies: An Interdisciplinary Forum on Subjective Well-Being, 4*(4), 385-404.

Agrawal, S., & Harter, J. (2010). *Relationship between perceived importance of wellbeing dimensions and overall wellbeing.* Gallup technical report.

Campbell, W. K., Krusemark, E. A., Dyckman, K. A., Brunell, A. B., McDowell, J. E., Twenge, J. M., & Clementz, B. A. (2006). A magnetoencephalography investigation of neural correlates for social exclusion and self-control. *Social Neuroscience, 1*(2), 124-134.

Canli, T., Qiu, M., Omura, K., Congdon, E., Haas, B. W., Amin, Z., Herrmann, M. J., Constable, R. T., & Lesch, K. P. (2006). Neural correlates of epigenesis. *PNAS, 103*(43), 16033-16038.

Christakis, N. A., & Fowler, J. H. (2009). *Connected: The surprising power of our social networks and how they shape our lives.* Little, Brown.

Christakis, N. A., & Fowler, J. H. (2013). Social contagion theory: Examining dynamic social networks and human behavior. *Statistics in Medicine, 32*(4), 556-577.

Davidson, R. J. (2005). Emotion regulation, happiness, and the neuroplasticity of the brain. *Advances in Mind-Body Medicine, 21*(3-4), 25-28.

De Neve, J. E., Krekel, C., & Ward, G. (2020). Work and well-being: A global perspective. In Helliwell, J., Layard, R., Sachs, J. D., & De Neve, J. E. (Eds.), *World happiness report 2020* (pp. 74-112). Sustainable Development Solutions Network. https://happiness-report.s3.amazonaws.com/2020/WHR20.pdf

Diener, E., & Biswas-Diener, R. (2011). *Happiness: Unlocking the mysteries of psychological wealth.* Wiley-Blackwell.

Emmons, R. A., & Diener, E. (1985). Personality correlates of subjective well-being. *Personality and Social Psychology Bulletin, 11*(1), 89-97.

Fujita, F., & Diener, E. (2005). Life satisfaction set point: stability and change. *Journal of Personality and Social Psychology, 88*(1), 158-164.

Gallup. (2012). *Do the five wellbeing elements predict life, work, and health outcomes or vice versa?* Gallup paper.

Harter, J. (2020, June 26). *If your employees aren't thriving, your business is struggling.* Gallup. https://www.gallup.com/workplace/313067/employees-aren-thriving-business-struggling.aspx

Harter, J. K., & Agrawal, S. (2012). *Causal relationships among wellbeing elements and life, work, and health outcomes.* Gallup technical report.

Helliwell, J., Layard, R., Sachs, J. D., & De Neve, J. E. (Eds.). (2020). *World happiness report 2020.* Sustainable Development Solutions Network. https://happiness-report.s3.amazonaws.com/2020/WHR20.pdf

Jablonka, E., & Raz, G. (2009). Transgenerational epigenetic inheritance: prevalence, mechanisms, and implications for the study of heredity and evolution. *The Quarterly Review of Biology, 84*(2), 131-176.

Jackson, M. O. (2009). Networks and economic behavior. *Annual Review of Economics, 1*(1), 489-511.

Judge, T. A., Locke, E. A., Durham, C. C., & Kluger, A. N. (1998). Dispositional effects on job and life satisfaction: The role of core evaluations. *Journal of Applied Psychology, 83*(1), 17-34.

Layard, R. (2011). *Happiness: Lessons from a new science.* Penguin.

Rath, T., & Harter, J. (2012). *The economics of wellbeing.* Gallup paper.

Wigert, B. (2020, March 13). *Employee burnout: The biggest myth.* Gallup. https://www.gallup.com/workplace/288539/employee-burnout-biggest-myth.aspx

Witters, D., & Agrawal, S. (2014, July 7). *What your workplace wellness programs are missing.* Gallup. https://news.gallup.com/businessjournal/172106/workplace-wellness-programs-missing.aspx

Career Wellbeing: You Like What You Do Every Day

Clifton, J., & Harter, J. (2019). *It's the manager.* Gallup Press.

Goh, J., Pfeffer, J., & Zenios, S. A. (2016). The relationship between workplace stressors and mortality and health costs in the United States. *Management Science, 62*(2), 608-628.

Harter, J. (2012, July 23). *Mondays not so "blue" for engaged employees.* Gallup. https://news.gallup.com/poll/155924/Mondays-Not-Blue-Engaged-Employees.aspx

Harter, J., & Stone, A. (2008, March 6-8). *The connection between work engagement and physiologic outcomes.* Work, Stress, and Health 2008: Health and Safe Work Through Research, Practice, and Partnerships. Washington, D.C.

Harter, J. K., & Stone, A. A. (2012). Engaging and disengaging work conditions, momentary experiences and cortisol response. *Motivation and Emotion, 36*(2), 104-113.

Krueger, A. B., Kahneman, D., Schkade, D., Schwarz, N., & Stone, A. A. (2009). National time accounting: The currency of life. In A. B. Krueger (Ed.), *Measuring the subjective well-being of nations: National accounts of time use and well-being* (pp. 9-86). University of Chicago Press.

McDaid, D., & Cooper, C. (Eds.). (2014). *Wellbeing: A complete reference guide, economics of wellbeing.* Wiley-Blackwell.

Pfeffer, J. (2018). *Dying for a paycheck: How modern management harms employee health and company performance — and what we can do about it.* HarperCollins Publishers.

Robertson, J., & Barling, J. (2014). Lead well, be well: Leadership behaviors influence employee wellbeing. In P. Y. Chen & C. L. Cooper (Eds.), *Wellbeing: A complete reference guide, work and wellbeing* (pp. 235-251). Wiley-Blackwell.

Social Wellbeing: You Have Meaningful Friendships in Your Life

Agrawal, S., & Harter, J. (2010). *How much does the wellbeing of others in the same household influence our own wellbeing?* Gallup paper.

Berkman, L. F. (1985). The relationship of social networks and social support to morbidity and mortality. In S. Cohen & S. L. Syme (Eds.), *Social Support and Health* (pp. 241-262). Academic Press.

Berkman, L. F. (1986). Social networks, support, and health: Taking the next step forward. *American Journal of Epidemiology, 123*(4), 559-562.

Berkman, L. F., & Syme, S. L. (1979). Social networks, host resistance, and mortality: a nine-year follow-up study of Alameda County residents. *American Journal of Epidemiology, 109*(2), 186-204.

Brim, B. J., & Williams, D. (2020, April 21). *Defeat employee loneliness and worry with CliftonStrengths.* Gallup. https://www.gallup.com/cliftonstrengths/en/308939/defeat-employee-loneliness-worry-cliftonstrengths.aspx

Christakis, N. A., & Fowler, J. H. (2009). *Connected: The surprising power of our social networks and how they shape our lives.* Little, Brown.

Christakis, N. A., & Fowler, J. H. (2013). Social contagion theory: Examining dynamic social networks and human behavior. *Statistics in Medicine, 32*(4), 556-577.

Gallup. (2016). *How millennials want to work and live.* Gallup paper.

Helliwell, J. F., & Wang, S. (2015). How was the weekend? How the social context underlies weekend effects in happiness and other emotions for US workers. *PLOS ONE, 10*(12), e0145123.

Norman, J. (2017, September 12). *Americans' ratings of standard of living best in decade.* Gallup. https://news.gallup.com/poll/218981/americans-ratings-standard-living-best-decade.aspx

Rigoni, B., & Nelson, B. (2016, November 8). *For millennials, is job-hopping inevitable?* Gallup. https://news.gallup.com/businessjournal/197234/millennials-job-hopping-inevitable.aspx

Financial Wellbeing: You Manage Your Money Well

Deaton, A. (2007). *Income, aging, health and wellbeing around the world: Evidence from the Gallup World Poll.* Princeton University Center for Health and Wellbeing Research Program in Development Studies and National Bureau of Economic Research.

Dunn, E. W., Aknin, L. B., & Norton, M. I. (2008). Spending money on others promotes happiness. *Science, 319*(5870), 1687-1688.

Fischer, R., & Boer, D. (2011). What is more important for national well-being: Money or autonomy? A meta-analysis of well-being, burnout, and anxiety across 63 societies. *Journal of Personality and Social Psychology, 101*(1), 164-184.

Gallup's perspective on how to align your employee compensation and talent management strategies. (2018). Gallup. https://www.gallup.com/workplace/248165/rewards-incentives-perspective-paper.aspx

How employee pay is perceived and why perception matters. (2017, July 28). PayScale. https://www.payscale.com/compensation-today/2017/07/employee-pay-perceived-perception-matters

Johnson, E. J., & Goldstein, D. (2003). Medicine. Do defaults save lives? *Science, 302*(5649), 1338-1339.

Kahneman, D., & Deaton, A. (2010). High income improves evaluation of life but not emotional well-being. *PNAS, 107*(38), 16489-16493.

Nessmith, W. E., Utkus, S. P., & Young, J. A. (2007) *Measuring the effectiveness of automatic enrollment.* Vanguard Center for Retirement Research.

Orszag, P. (2008, August 7). *Behavioral economics: Lessons from retirement research for health care and beyond.* Retirement Research Consortium.

Probst, T. M., Sinclair, R. R., Sears, L. E., Gailey, N. J., Black, K. J., & Cheung, J. H. (2018). Economic stress and well-being: Does population health context matter? *Journal of Applied Psychology, 103*(9), 959-979.

Rath, T., & Harter, J. *The economics of wellbeing.* Gallup paper.

Rigoni, B., & Nelson, B. (2016, January 15). *Retaining employees: How much does money matter?* Gallup. https://news.gallup.com/businessjournal/188399/retaining-employees-money-matter.aspx

San Francisco State University. (2009, February 17). *Buying experiences, not possessions, leads to greater happiness.* ScienceDaily. www.sciencedaily.com/releases/2009/02/090207150518.htm

Solnick, S. J., & Hemenway, D. (1998). Is more always better?: A survey on positional concerns. *Journal of Economic Behavior & Organization, 37*(3), 373-383.

State of the American workplace report. (2017). Gallup. https://www.gallup.com/workplace/238085/state-american-workplace-report-2017.aspx

Thaler, R. H. (1999). Mental accounting matters. *Journal of Behavioral Decision Making, 12*(3), 183-206.

Willis Tower Watson. *2017/2018 Global Benefits Attitudes Survey.* Survey Report.

Physical Wellbeing: You Have Energy to Get Things Done

Background: The Affordable Care Act's new rules on preventive care. (2020). CMS.gov. https://www.cms.gov/CCIIO/Resources/Fact-Sheets-and-FAQs/preventive-care-background

Besedovsky, L., Lange, T., & Haack, M. (2019). The sleep-immune crosstalk in health and disease. *Physiological Reviews, 99*(3), 1325-1380.

Boespflug, E. L., & Iliff, J. J. (2018). The emerging relationship between interstitial fluid-cerebrospinal fluid exchange, amyloid-β, and sleep. *Biological Psychiatry, 83*(4), 328-336.

Cassilhas, R. C., Tufik, S., & de Mello, M. T. (2016). Physical exercise, neuroplasticity, spatial learning and memory. *Cellular and Molecular Life Sciences, 73*(5), 975-983.

Christ, A., Lauterbach, M., & Latz, E. (2019). Western diet and the immune system: An inflammatory connection. *Immunity, 51*(5), 794-811.

Cohen, S., Doyle, W. J., Alper, C. M., Janicki-Deverts, D., & Turner, R. B. (2009). Sleep habits and susceptibility to the common cold. *Archives of Internal Medicine, 169*(1), 62-67.

De Souza, R. J., Mente, A., Maroleanu, A., Cozma, A. I., Ha, V., Kishibe, T., Uleryk, E., Budylowski, P., Schunemann, H., Beyene, J., & Anand, S. S. (2015). Intake of saturated and trans unsaturated fatty acids and risk of all cause mortality, cardiovascular disease, and type 2 diabetes: Systematic review and meta-analysis of observational studies. *BMJ, 351*, h3978.

Ellis, R. (2020, August 18). *COVID the third-leading cause of death in the U.S.* WebMD. https://www.webmd.com/lung/news/20200818/covid-the-third-leading-cause-of-death-in-the-us

Gangwisch, J. E. (2014). A review of evidence for the link between sleep duration and hypertension. *American Journal of Hypertension, 27*(10), 1235-1242.

Gleeson, M. (2007). Immune function in sport and exercise. *Journal of Applied Physiology, 103*(2), 693-699.

Hafner, M., Stepanek, M., Taylor, J., Troxel, W. M., & van Stolk, C. (2017). Why sleep matters — the economic costs of insufficient sleep: A cross-country comparative analysis. *Rand Health Quarterly, 6*(4), 11.

Hansen, C. J., Stevens, L. C., & Coast, J. R. (2001). Exercise duration and mood state: How much is enough to feel better? *Health Psychology, 20*(4), 267-275.

Hoffman, M. D., & Hoffman, D. R. (2008). Exercisers achieve greater acute exercise-induced mood enhancement than nonexercisers. *Archives of Physical Medicine and Rehabilitation, 89*(2), 358-363.

Imamura, F., Micha, R., Wu, J. H. Y., de Oliveira Otto, M. C., Otite, F. O., Abioye, A. I., & Mozaffarian, D. (2016). Effects of saturated fat, polyunsaturated fat, monounsaturated fat, and carbohydrate on glucose-insulin homeostasis: A systematic review and meta-analysis of randomised controlled feeding trials. *PLOS Medicine, 13*(7), e1002087.

Jike, M., Itani, O., Watanabe, N., Buysse, D. J., & Kaneita, Y. (2018). Long sleep duration and health outcomes: A systematic review, meta-analysis and meta-regression. *Sleep Medicine Reviews, 39*, 25-36.

Jowsey, J. (1971). Bone at the cellular level: The effects of inactivity. In Murray R. H., McCalley, M. (Eds.), *Hypogravic and Hypodynamic Environments* (pp. 111-119). NASA.

Kim, Y., & Je, Y. (2014). Dietary fiber intake and total mortality: A meta-analysis of prospective cohort studies. *American Journal of Epidemiology, 180*(6), 565-573.

Kritchevsky. D. (1998). History of recommendations to the public about dietary fat. *The Journal of Nutrition, 128*(2), 449S-452S.

La Berge, A. F. (2008). How the ideology of low fat conquered America. *Journal of the History of Medicine and Allied Sciences, 63*(2), 139-177.

Martin, A., Fitzsimons, C., Jepson, R., Saunders, D. H., van der Ploeg, H. P., Teixeira, P. J., Gray, C. M., Mutrie, N., & EuroFIT Consortium. (2015). Interventions with potential to reduce sedentary time in adults: Systematic review and meta-analysis. *British Journal of Sports Medicine, 49*(16), 1056-1063.

O'Boyle, E., & Harter, J. (2014, May 13). *Why your workplace wellness program isn't working.* Gallup. https://www.gallup.com/workplace/236531/why-workplace-wellness-program-isn-working.aspx

Rath, T., & Harter, J. (2010). *Wellbeing: The five essential elements.* Gallup Press.

Remig, V., Franklin, B., Margolis, S., Kostas, G., Nece, T., & Street, J. C. (2010). Trans fats in America: A review of their use, consumption, health implications, and regulation. *Journal of the American Dietetic Association, 110*(4), 585-592.

Seidelmann, S. B., Claggett, B., Cheng, S., Henglin, M., Shah, A., Steffen, L. M., Folsom, A.R., Rimm, E. B., & Solomon, S. D. (2018). Dietary carbohydrate intake and mortality: A prospective cohort study and meta-analysis. *The Lancet Public Health, 3*(9), e419-e428.

Simpson, R. J., Lowder, T. W., Spielmann, G., Bigley, A. B., LaVoy, E. C., & Kunz, H. (2012). Exercise and the aging immune system. *Ageing Research Reviews, 11*(3), 404-420.

Swaminathan, N. (2008, April 29). *Why does the brain need so much power?* Scientific American. https://www.scientificamerican.com/article/why-does-the-brain-need-s/

Wang, Y., Mei, H., Jiang, Y. R., Sun, W. Q., Song, Y. J., Liu, S. J., & Jiang, F. (2015). Relationship between duration of sleep and hypertension in adults: A meta-analysis. *Journal of Clinical Sleep Medicine, 11*(9), 1047-1056.

Witters, D., & Agrawal, S. (2020, March 27). *11 million in U.S. at serious risk if infected with COVID-19.* Gallup. https://news.gallup.com/poll/304643/million-severe-risk-infected-covid.aspx

Xie, L., Kang, H., Xu, Q., Chen, M. J., Liao, Y., Thiyagarajan, M., O'Donnell, J., Cristensen, D. J., Nicholson, C., Iliff, J. J., Takano, T., Deane, R., & Nedergaard, N. (2013). Sleep drives metabolite clearance from the adult brain. *Science, 342*(6156), 373-377.

Youngstedt, S. D., Goff, E. E., Reynolds, A. M., Kripke, D. F., Irwin, M. R., Bootzin, R. R., Khan, N., & Jean-Louis, G. (2016). Has adult sleep duration declined over the last 50+ years? *Sleep Medicine Reviews, 28*, 69-85.

Community Wellbeing: You Like Where You Live

Davies, P. A., Dudek, P. M., & Wyatt, K. S. (2020). Recent developments in ESG reporting. In Esty, D. C., Cort, T. (Eds.), *Values at Work* (pp. 161-179). Palgrave Macmillan.

Hillyer, M. (2020, September 22). *Measuring stakeholder capitalism: Top global companies take action on universal ESG reporting.* World Economic Forum. https://www.weforum.org/press/2020/09/measuring-stakeholder-capitalism-top-global-companies-take-action-on-universal-esg-reporting

Le, B. M., Impett, E. A., Lemay, E. P., Muise, A., & Tskhay, K. O. (2018). Communal motivation and well-being in interpersonal relationships: An integrative review and meta-analysis. *Psychological Bulletin, 144*(1), 1-25.

Orlitzky, M., Schmidt, F. L., & Rynes, S. L. (2003). Corporate social and financial performance: A meta-analysis. *Organization Studies, 24*(3), 403-441.

Post, S. G. (2005). Altruism, happiness, and health: It's good to be good. *International Journal of Behavioral Medicine, 12*(2), 66-77.

Wang, Q., Dou, J., & Jia, S. (2016). A meta-analytic review of corporate social responsibility and corporate financial performance: The moderating effect of contextual factors. *Business & Society, 55*(8), 1083-1121.

How to Build a Culture of Net Thriving

Bassuk, S. S., Church, T. S., & Manson, J. E. (2013). Researchers explain why exercise works magic. *Scientific American, 309*(2), 74-79.

Christakis, N. A., & Fowler, J. H. (2009). *Connected: The surprising power of our social networks and how they shape our lives.* Little, Brown.

Dunn, E. W., Aknin, L. B., & Norton, M. I. (2008). Spending money on others promotes happiness. *Science, 319*(5870), 1687-1688.

Dunn, E. W., Aknin, L. B., & Norton, M. I. (2014). Prosocial spending and happiness: Using money to benefit others pays off. *Current Directions in Psychological Science, 23*(1), 41-47.

Harter, J., & Agrawal, S. *Social time: With whom we spend it, what we do, and its impact on our mood.* Gallup research study.

Nessmith, W. E., Utkus, S. P., & Young, J. A. (2007) *Measuring the effectiveness of automatic enrollment.* Vanguard Center for Retirement Research.

Piliavin, J. A. (2003). Doing well by doing good: Benefits for the benefactor. In C. L. M. Keyes & J. Haidt (Eds.), *Flourishing: Positive psychology and the life well-lived* (pp. 227-247). American Psychological Association.

Stone, A., & Harter, J. *The experience of work: A momentary perspective. A collaboration between Gallup, Stony Brook University, Princeton University, and Syracuse University.* Research study.

Thaler, R. H. (1999). Mental accounting matters. *Journal of Behavioral Decision Making, 12*(3), 183-206.

Thorén, P., Floras, J. S., Hoffmann, P., & Seals, D. R. (1990). Endorphins and exercise: Physiological mechanisms and clinical implications. *Medicine & Science in Sports & Exercise, 22*(4), 417-428.

Part 3: Risks to a Net Thriving Culture

Risk #1: Employee Mental Health

Agrawal, S., & Harter, J. (2009). *Engagement at work predicts changes in depression and anxiety status in the next year.* Gallup report.

Asplund, J., Leibbrandt, M., & Robison, J. (2020, June 9). *How strengths, wellbeing and engagement reduce burnout.* Gallup. https://www.gallup.com/cliftonstrengths/en/312467/strengths-wellbeing-engagement-reduce-burnout.aspx

Case, A., & Deaton, A. (2015). Rising morbidity and mortality in midlife among White non-Hispanic Americans in the 21st century. *PNAS, 112*(49), 15078-15083.

Case, A., & Deaton, A. (2017). Mortality and morbidity in the 21st century. *Brookings Papers on Economic Activity, 2017*(1), 397-476.

Case, A., & Deaton, A. (2020). *Deaths of despair and the future of capitalism.* Princeton University Press.

Clark, A. E. (2010). Work, jobs, and well-being across the millennium. In E. Diener, J. F. Helliwell, & D. Kahneman (Eds.), *International differences in well-being* (pp. 436-468). Oxford University Press.

Demakakos, P., Biddulph, J. P., de Oliveira, C., Tsakos, G., & Marmot, M. G. (2018). Subjective social status and mortality: The English longitudinal study of ageing. *European Journal of Epidemiology, 33*(8), 729-739.

English Longitudinal Study of Ageing (ELSA). (n.d.). ELSA. https://www.elsa-project.ac.uk/

Herbert, T. B., & Cohen, S. (1993). Stress and immunity in humans: A meta-analysis review. *Psychosomatic Medicine, 55*(4), 364-379.

Jones, J. M. (2020, June 22). *In U.S., negative emotions surged, then declined in June.* Gallup. https://news.gallup.com/poll/312872/negative-emotions-surged-declined-june.aspx

Witters, D., & Harter, J. (2020, May 8). *Worry and stress fuel record drop in U.S. life satisfaction.* Gallup. https://news.gallup.com/poll/310250/worry-stress-fuel-record-drop-life-satisfaction.aspx

Risk #2: Lack of Clarity and Purpose

(2019). *Fit for the future: An urgent imperative for board leadership.* NACD. https://nacdonline.org/insights/blue_ribbon.cfm?ItemNumber=66336

Clifton, J., & Harter, J. (2019). *It's the manager.* Gallup Press.

Gallup. (n.d.). *The manager experience: Pros, cons and development opportunities.* Gallup. https://www.gallup.com/workplace/321074/perks-and-challenges-of-management.aspx#ite-321491

Gallup. (2019). *Gallup's perspective series on the manager experience: Top challenges & perks of managers.* Gallup paper.

Harter, J. (2019, June 13). *Why some leaders have their employees' trust, and some don't.* Gallup. https://www.gallup.com/workplace/258197/why-leaders-employees-trust-don.aspx

Risk #3: Overreliance on Policies, Programs and Perks

Anand, R., & Winters, M. (2008). A retrospective view of corporate diversity training from 1964 to the present. *Academy of Management Learning & Education, 7*(3), 356-372.

Astrella, J. A. (2017). Return on investment: Evaluating the evidence regarding financial outcomes of workplace wellness programs. *JONA, 47*(7-8), 379-383.

Bezrukova, K., Spell, C. S., Perry, J. L., & Jehn, K. A. (2016). A meta-analytical integration of over 40 years of research on diversity training evaluation. *Psychological Bulletin, 142*(2), 1227-1274.

Clifton, J., & Harter, J. (2019). *It's the manager.* Gallup Press.

Downey, S. N., van der Werff, L., Thomas, K. M., & Plaut, V. C. (2015). The role of diversity practices and inclusion in promoting trust and employee engagement. *Journal of Applied Social Psychology, 45*(1), 35-44.

Gallup. (n.d.). *Working remotely: Careers, management and strategy.* Gallup. https://www.gallup.com/workplace/316313/understanding-and-managing-remote-workers.aspx#ite-316397

Gallup. (2016). *How millennials want to work and live.* Gallup paper.

Gallup. (2018). *Three requirements of a diverse and inclusive culture — and why they matter for your organization.* Gallup paper.

Gallup. (2020). *Gallup's perspective on the evolution of remote work amid COVID-19.* Gallup paper.

Goetzel, R. Z., Henke, R. M., Tabrizi, M., Pelletier, K. R., Loeppke, R., Ballard, D. W., Grossmeier, J., Anderson, D. R., Yach, D., Kelly, R. K., McCalister, T., Serxner, S., Selecky, C., Shallenberger, L. G., Fries, J. F., Baase, C., Isaac, F., Crighton, K. A., Wald, P., & Metz, R. D. (2014). Do workplace health promotion (wellness) programs work? *Journal of Occupational and Environmental Medicine, 56*(9), 927-934.

Harter, J. (2014, September 9). *Should employers ban email after work hours?* Gallup. https://www.gallup.com/workplace/236519/employers-ban-email-work-hours.aspx

Harter, J. K., & Agrawal, S. (April 2012). *Engagement at work: Working hours, flextime, vacation time, and well-being.* Gallup report.

Harter, J. K., & Arora, R. (2008). *The impact of time spent working and job fit on well-being around the world.* Gallup paper.

Hickman, A., & Saad, L. (2020, May 22). *Reviewing remote work in the U.S. under COVID-19.* Gallup. https://news.gallup.com/poll/311375/reviewing-remote-work-covid.aspx

London, M., Polzer, J. T., & Omoregie, H. (2005). Interpersonal congruence, transactive memory, and feedback processes: An integrative model of group learning. *Human Resource Development Review, 4*(2), 114-135.

O'Boyle, E., & Harter, J. (2014, May 13). *Why your workplace wellness program isn't working.* Gallup. https://www.gallup.com/workplace/236531/why-workplace-wellness-program-isn-working.aspx

Robison, J. (2012, December 18). *For employee well-being, engagement trumps time off.* Gallup. https://news.gallup.com/businessjournal/159374/employee-wellbeing-engagement-trumps-time-off.aspx

Wigert, B., & Harter, J. (2017). *Re-engineering performance management.* Gallup paper.

Risk #4: Poorly Skilled Managers

Clifton, J., & Harter, J. (2019). *It's the manager.* Gallup Press.

Gallup. (2020). *Gallup's perspective on the evolution of remote work amid COVID-19.* Gallup paper.

O'Boyle, E., & Harter, J. (2014, May 13). *Why your workplace wellness program isn't working.* Gallup. https://www.gallup.com/workplace/236531/why-workplace-wellness-program-isn-working.aspx

Wigert, B., & Harter, J. (2017). *Re-engineering performance management.* Gallup paper.

Resilient Cultures in a Crisis

The share of adults reporting symptoms of anxiety or depression ballooned during the 2020 pandemic, according to data from the National Center for

Health Statistics and the U.S. Census Bureau, rising to 40.9% by mid-July. A similar national survey from the first half of 2019 put that number at 11%.

(2020, April 23-July 21). Anxiety and depression: Household pulse survey. National Center for Health Statistics. https://www.cdc.gov/nchs/covid19/pulse/mental-health.htm

Gallup. (2008). *Strengths based leadership: Great leaders, teams, and why people follow.* Gallup Press.

Harter, J., & Agrawal, S. (2011, March 30). *Workers in bad jobs have worse well-being than jobless.* Gallup. https://news.gallup.com/poll/146867/Workers-Bad-Jobs-Worse-Wellbeing-Jobless.aspx

Harter, J. K., Schmidt, F. L., Agrawal, S., Plowman, S. K., & Blue, A. T. (2020). Increased business value for positive job attitudes during economic recessions: A meta-analysis and SEM analysis. *Human Performance, 33*(4), 307-330.

Part 4: Net Thriving Starts With Career Engagement

The Largest Study of Its Kind

Edmans, A. (2012). The link between job satisfaction and firm value, with implications for corporate social responsibility. *Academy of Management Perspectives, 26*(4), 1-19.

Harrison, D. A., Newman, D. A., & Roth, P. L. (2006). How important are job attitudes? Meta-analytic comparisons of integrative behavioral outcomes and time sequences. *Academy of Management Journal, 49*(2), 305-325.

Krekel, C., Ward G., & De Neve, J. E. (2019). Employee well-being, productivity, and firm performance: Evidence and case studies. In *Global Happiness and Wellbeing Policy Report 2019* (pp. 72-94). Sustainable Development Solutions Network. https://s3.amazonaws.com/ghwbpr-2019/UAE/GH19_Ch5.pdf

Mackay, M. M., Allen, J. A., & Landis, R. S. (2017). Investigating the incremental validity of employee engagement in the prediction of employee effectiveness: A meta-analytic path analysis. *Human Resource Management Review, 27*(1), 108-120.

Whitman, D. S., Van Rooy, D. L., & Viswesvaran, C. (2010). Satisfaction, citizenship behaviors, and performance in work units: A meta-analysis of collective construct relations. *Personnel Psychology, 63*(1), 41-81.

Adopting Wellbeing Practices

Helliwell, J. F., & Huang, H. (2011). Well-being and trust in the workplace. *Journal of Happiness Studies, 12*(5), 747-767.

O'Boyle, E., & Harter, J. (2014, May 13). *Why your workplace wellness program isn't working.* Gallup. https://www.gallup.com/workplace/236531/why-workplace-wellness-program-isn-working.aspx

Thompson, S. E., Smith, B. A., & Bybee, R. F. (2005). Factors influencing participation in worksite wellness programs among minority and underserved populations. *Family & Community Health, 28*(3), 267-273.

My Expectations

Berman, S. L., Down, J., & Hill, C. W. (2002). Tacit knowledge as a source of competitive advantage in the National Basketball Association. *Academy of Management Journal, 45*(1), 13-31.

Clifton, J., & Harter, J. (2019). *It's the manager.* Gallup Press.

DeChurch, L. A., & Mesmer-Magnus, J. R. (2010). The cognitive underpinnings of effective teamwork: A meta-analysis. *Journal of Applied Psychology, 95*(1), 32-53.

Edmondson, A. C., Winslow, A. B., Bohmer, R. M., & Pisano, G. P. (2003). Learning how and learning what: Effects of tacit and codified knowledge on performance improvement following technology adoption. *Decision Sciences, 34*(2), 197-224.

Gallup. (2019). *Gallup's perspective series on the manager experience: Top challenges & perks of managers.* Gallup paper.

Kleingeld, A., van Mierlo, H., & Arends, L. (2011). The effect of goal setting on group performance: A meta-analysis. *Journal of Applied Psychology, 96*(6), 1289-1304.

Mathieu, J. E., Hollenbeck, J. R., van Knippenberg, D., & Ilgen, D. R. (2017). A century of work teams in the *Journal of Applied Psychology. Journal of Applied Psychology, 102*(3), 452-467.

Tubre, T. C., & Collins, J. M. (2000). Jackson and Schuler (1985) revisited: A meta-analysis of the relationships between role ambiguity, role conflict, and job performance. *Journal of Management, 26*(1), 155-169.

Woolley, A. W., Aggarwal, I., & Malone, T. W. (2015). Collective intelligence and group performance. *Current Directions in Psychological Science, 24*(6), 420-424.

My Strengths

Csikszentmihalyi, M. (1998). *Finding flow: The psychology of engagement with everyday life.* Basic Books.

Csikszentmihalyi, M. (2013). *Creativity: Flow and the psychology of discovery and invention.* HarperCollins.

Harter, J. K., & Stone, A. A. (2012). Engaging and disengaging work conditions, momentary experiences and cortisol response. *Motivation and Emotion, 36*(2), 104-113.

Kristof-Brown, A. L., Zimmerman, R. D., & Johnson, E. C. (2005). Consequences of individual's fit at work: A meta-analysis of person-job, person-organization, person-group, and person-supervisor fit. *Personnel Psychology, 58*(2), 281-342.

Stone, A., & Harter, J. (2009). *The experience of work: A momentary perspective. A collaboration between Gallup, Stony Brook University, Princeton University, and Syracuse University.* Research study.

My Development

Eby, L. T., Allen, T. D., Evans, S. C., Ng, T., & DuBois, D. L. (2008). Does mentoring matter? A multidisciplinary meta-analysis comparing mentored and non-mentored individuals. *Journal of Vocational Behavior, 72*(2), 254-267.

Jiang, K., Lepak, D. P., Hu, J., & Baer, J. C. (2012). How does human resource management influence organizational outcomes? A meta-analytic investigation of mediating mechanisms. *Academy of Management Journal, 55*(6), 1264-1294.

Kluger, A. N., & DeNisi, A. (1996). The effects of feedback interventions on performance: A historical review, a meta-analysis, and a preliminary feedback intervention theory. *Psychological Bulletin, 119*(2), 254-284.

Latham, G. P., & Locke, E. A. (2007). New developments in and directions for goal-setting research. *European Psychologist, 12*(4), 290-300.

Lockwood, P., Jordan, C. H., & Kunda, Z. (2002). Motivation by positive or negative role models: Regulatory focus determines who will best inspire us. *Journal of Personality and Social Psychology, 83*(4), 854-864.

Wigert, B., & Maese, E. (2019, July 8). *Why manager development programs aren't working.* Gallup. https://www.gallup.com/workplace/259466/why-manager-development-programs-aren-working.aspx

My Opinions

Brown, S. P. (1996). A meta-analysis and review of organizational research on job involvement. *Psychological Bulletin, 120*(2), 235-255.

Clifton, J., & Harter, J. (2019). *It's the manager.* Gallup Press.

Kivimäki, M., Ferrie, J. E., Brunner, E., Head, J., Shipley, M. J., Vahtera, J., & Marmot, M. G. (2005). Justice at work and reduced risk of coronary heart disease among employees: The Whitehall II study. *Archives of Internal Medicine, 165*(19), 2245-2251.

Marmot, M. G. (2006). Status syndrome: A challenge to medicine. *JAMA, 295*(11), 1304-1307.

Spector, P. E. (1986). Perceived control by employees: A meta-analysis of studies concerning autonomy and participation at work. *Human Relations, 39*(11), 1005-1016.

My Mission or Purpose

Cerasoli, C. P., Nicklin, J. M., & Ford, M. T. (2014). Intrinsic motivation and extrinsic incentives jointly predict performance: A 40-year meta-analysis. *Psychological Bulletin, 140*(4), 980-1008.

Gartenberg, C., Prat, A., & Serafeim, G. (2019). Corporate purpose and financial performance. *Organization Science, 30*(1), 1-18.

Podsakoff, N. P., Whiting, S. W., Podsakoff, P. M., & Blume, B. D. (2009). Individual- and organizational-level consequences of organizational citizenship behaviors: A meta-analysis. *Journal of Applied Psychology, 94*(1), 122-141.

Part 5: The Fastest Road to Net Thriving: Play to Strengths

Strengths Make Wellbeing Work

Asplund, J., Harter, J. K., Agrawal, S., & Plowman, S. K. (2015). *The relationship between strengths-based employee development and organizational outcomes: 2015 strengths meta-analysis.* Gallup paper.

Clifton, D. O., & Harter, J. K. (2003). Investing in strengths. In A. K. S. Cameron, B. J. E. Dutton, & C. R. E. Quinn (Eds.), *Positive Organizational Scholarship: Foundations of a New Discipline* (pp. 111-121). Berrett-Koehler.

Clifton, D. O., & Nelson, P. (1996). *Soar with your strengths*. Dell Books.

Gallup. (2001). *Now, discover your strengths*. Simon & Schuster.

Gallup. (2007). *StrengthsFinder 2.0*. Gallup Press

About Gallup

Gallup is a global analytics, advisory and learning firm that helps leaders solve their organizations' biggest problems.

Gallup knows more about the will of employees, customers, students and citizens than any other organization in the world. We offer solutions, transformations and services in many areas, including:

- Culture change
- Leadership development
- Manager development
- Strengths-based coaching and culture
- Strategies for organic growth
- "Boss-to-coach" software tools
- Attracting and recruiting star team members
- Succession planning
- Performance management system and ratings
- Refining performance metrics

- Reducing defects and safety risks
- Evaluating internal programs
- Employee engagement and experience
- Predictive hiring assessments
- Retention forecasting
- Creating agile teams
- Improving the customer experience (B2B)
- Diversity and inclusion
- Wellbeing initiatives

To learn more, please contact Gallup at https://www.gallup.com/contact.

About the Authors

Jim Clifton

Jim Clifton is Chairman and CEO of Gallup and bestselling author of *The Coming Jobs War*, *Born to Build* and the #1 *Wall Street Journal* bestseller *It's the Manager*. One of his most significant innovations, the Gallup World Poll, is designed to give the world's 7 billion citizens a voice in virtually all key global issues. Under Clifton's leadership, Gallup has expanded from a predominantly U.S.-based company to a worldwide organization with 40 offices in 30 countries and regions. Clifton is currently a Distinguished Visiting Professor and Senior Fellow of the Frank Hawkins Kenan Institute of Private Enterprise at the University of North Carolina.

Jim Harter

Jim Harter, Ph.D., is Chief Scientist, Workplace for Gallup. He has led more than 1,000 studies of workplace effectiveness, including the largest ongoing meta-analysis of human potential and business unit performance. The bestselling author of *12: The Elements of Great Managing*, *Wellbeing: The Five Essential Elements* and the #1 *Wall Street Journal* bestseller *It's the Manager*, Harter has also published articles in many prominent business and academic journals.

Acknowledgements

Wellbeing at Work is the product of decades of work conducted by Gallup scientists, consultants, client organizations and leading scientists from the academic community — based on the opinions and behaviors of 100 million employees from workplaces throughout the world. While we extracted findings and condensed them into this book, the following larger team provided direction, critical thinking, research and editorial guidance:

Editor: Geoff Brewer

Gallup Press publisher: Seth Schuchman

Chief of staff for Jim Clifton: Christine Sheehan

Copy editor: Kelly Henry

Fact checker: Trista Kunce

Designer: Samantha Allemang

Writing and editing contributions: Jim Asplund, Ryan Pendell, Jaclynn Robinson, Christine Sheehan, Austin Suellentrop

Administrative support: Carissa Christensen, Gayle Hoybook, Shawna Hubbard-Thomas

Writing for websites and marketing: Klayton Kasperbauer

Press coordinator: Christy Trout

Communications: Ashley Anderson

Technology: Emily Ternus

Science team: Sangeeta Agrawal, Jim Asplund, Kristin Barry, Anthony Blue, Kristy Carlson, Nate Dvorak, Cheryl Fernandez, Kiran Jha, Patrick Josh, Ellyn Maese, Emily Meyer, Marco Nink, Ryan Pendell, Stephanie Plowman, Puneet Singh, Dipak Sundaram, Anna Truscott-Smith, Emily Wetherell, Ben Wigert, Dan Witters

Peer review: Jim Asplund, Larry Emond, Dean Jones, Katie Lyon, Tom Matson, Jane Miller, Iseult Morgan, Ed O'Boyle, Steve O'Brien, Ken Royal, Ryan Shaughnessy, Pa Sinyan, Chris Stewart, Ben Wigert, Dan Witters, Ryan Wolf, John Wood

We wouldn't be here today without the extraordinary thought leadership of Nobel laureates Danny Kahneman and Angus Deaton.

Ed Diener, the most prolific wellbeing researcher in the world, has partnered with us for decades. His influence on the advanced science of wellbeing has been enormous.

For their partnership, we also thank Gallup Senior Scientists and Advisers Lisa Berkman, Mihaly Csikszentmihalyi, John Helliwell,

Jan-Emmanuel De Neve, Jeffrey Pfeffer, Frank Schmidt and Arthur Stone.

We thank George Gallup (1901-1984), Don Clifton (1924-2003) and Gale Muller (1944-2015) who, from Gallup's roots, pioneered the early science of wellbeing. Dr. Gallup, starting in the 1930s, designed the first methods for scientific sampling and spent his career studying "the will of the people." Dr. Clifton, the father of strengths-based psychology and inventor of the CliftonStrengths assessment, taught us all to study what is *right* with people. Dr. Muller engineered and built Gallup's famous World Poll — probably the greatest feat in the history of polling and survey research.

Special thanks to the girl at United Gate F4 and RaLinda.

Gallup Press exists to educate and inform the people who govern, manage, teach and lead the world's 7 billion citizens. Each book meets Gallup's requirements of integrity, trust and independence and is based on Gallup-approved science and research.